Widy

Love whispered with a smile

by Jody Hauf

You may be wondering how to pronounce Widy's name. It's WEE-DEE. The irony is, a boy with a name that sounds like a troubled garden, blossomed like a most beautiful flower along the highways and byways of life.

May his story inspire you to see the beauty that is all around us.

**MATER
MEDIA**

Published by Mater Media
St. Louis, Missouri
www.matermedia.org

Cover and Interior Design: Trese Gloriod
Editors: Cathy Gilmore, Kelly Boutross

Printed in the USA.

978-0-9913542-3-8

Acknowledgments

Writing Widy's story was a work of love and inspiration. So many people made this book possible.

First of all, I'd like to thank Almighty God for the gift of Widy to today's troubled world.

I'd like to thank my family for their encouragement and support, especially my husband, Bob, who was my greatest cheerleader. He kept me on task and encouraged me onward constantly.

I thank all those who read my many drafts and offered their suggestions. Without their help there would be no Widy's story. To Mary Weman, who read my very first feeble attempt: thank you, Mary, for not laughing at the mess, but giving me suggestions and encouragement to go forward with this story. To Carol Komor, David and Linda Straub, Stephanie Lombard, Denis and Linda Thien, Rita (my spiritual director), Zip Rzeppa, and a special thanks to Fr. Ed Hauf for reading and editing.

To the parishioners of Holy Infant for their support and encouragement.

A special thanks to the Holy Spirit for the inspiration and especially for not letting me give up on this endeavor. Thank you for continuing to whisper encouragement into my heart.

All for the glory of God

One child
precious child
broken, deformed, disabled
becomes God's doorway.
God's graces flow
people love
people share
people give
all for this precious child.

Precious child
broken, deformed, disabled
doorway for God's graces
people show God's love
people show God's generosity
people show God's goodness
all for the glory of God

To God be the glory
glory for all Your creation
glory and graciousness to allow us to see as You see
To see wholeness where the world sees brokenness
to see beauty where the world sees deformity
ability where the world sees disability
through Your eyes we see wholeness in You through our brokenness
beauty and wholeness in deformity
ability and courage in disability

You sent Widy into all our world
to show us Your great glory

Thank You for showing us your love and pouring out Your
graces on us by giving us Widy to see Your love and grace
in action

All for the glory of God
to God be the glory

Foreword

*"Go into the whole world and proclaim the gospel
to every creature." Mark 16:15*

In today's world so filled with discouragement, greed, and self-seeking relativism, Widy was an oasis—an island of peace that surpasses all understanding. He was joy in just being, just being a beloved creation of God. Widy never did any great, wonderful things, but he brought out great, wonderful goodness from everyone he touched. He reflected God's great love to all with whom he had contact. And they responded with great love— from the little boy in the swimming pool to kids gathered around his wheelchair singing with him, to the older lady who asked him to pray for her. He showed us all how to live as God created us to live. He was a Gospel to the world.

He showed the world how God creates each and every one of us as extraordinarily valuable in the beautiful, rich story God is writing through each of our lives. In the world today, especially through media, we see so much of the bad—the bad things people say and do. In Widy's short life, he brought out the good in people. He just exuded peace, joy and love. He showed me the goodness in people and how they reflected God's presence and beauty. I cried when Widy died. Of course I'd miss that smile, that courage and hope he brought to me. My cry was, "Now, who will teach me about God?" Widy was my living 'Good News.'

Let me share his story with you, that you, too, may be touched by God.

*"I am who I am in the eyes of God. Nothing more,
nothing less." (St. Francis of Assisi)*

Be Still

Be still and know that I am God.

Be still and know

Be still

Be

I often pray and meditate upon these words. Widy lived them out. Widy was a BE. I would say prayers with him each day. Morning prayers were, "Thank you, God for this new day." Bedtime prayers were for Mama Anne, his "Haiti Mama," his friends, etc. I would say the prayers and Widy would just look at me and smile. He didn't need words to speak to God, he listened to God. He was still. He was a BE. Widy's whole life was a prayer. He always was who he was in the eyes of God, nothing more, nothing less. He was teaching me how to pray, how to live. He was teaching me how to be a BE, to be who I am in the eyes of God—nothing more, nothing less.

I must do what I must do

The Holy Spirit has been whispering into my heart ever since Widy came into my life that I must tell his story. What I've written is what I've heard whispered in my soul during my daily prayer as I try to silence myself and listen to the soft whisper of the Holy Spirit.

This is not only Widy's story, it is God's story. The story of God touching my life, of God reaching into my everyday existence and connecting my life with myriads of other lives. It is a story of how God touches all our lives and weaves them together into a glorious tale of His love and grace. It is a story of how He touched me, and how He touched others and how others have touched me and we are all touched by the reality of God's existence; a story of how we all can give glory to God through our existence.

Widy whispers

Writing Widy's story has not been an easy task. Writing in simple chronological order doesn't work because his life took so many twists and turns that involved so many special people. I thank you for joining me on this journey that sometimes takes the scenic route, not speeding past the beautiful countryside that was such a refreshing gift amidst an otherwise often rocky, steep trek! Also, I write this story as if you were here beside me, as I reflect on Widy's life and love. If my writing style is too conversational, I ask your forgiveness.

I have placed a sort of "timeline" at the end of the book so you can see the context to know when particular events happened in relation to each other. As I wrote his story, I felt Widy was somehow whispering into my ear, little thoughts he wanted to express. I have included these thoughts in the form of "love letters" from him. My hope is that he will be able to whisper to your heart through what I share on these pages so you can experience Widy's love and life in a personal way, too.

"God is so awesome. He created me special so that I could show people how awesome He is. He loves all of us so much and wants each of us to know that love, and share that love, with others. I tried to do that in my life; to show the world how very many good people there are in the world, to give courage and hope to the world in my own little corner of it. After all, if each of us did that in our own little corners, there would be more hope and light in the world in which we live. I love you and above all God loves you."

Love, Widy

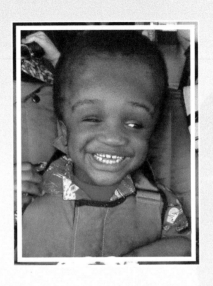

Trust in the Lord with all your heart,
On your own intelligence do not rely;
In all your ways be mindful of Him,
And He will make straight your paths.
Proverbs 3:5-6

I found another heart-shaped leaf today.

I remember vividly the crisp autumn day with its bright sun and the smell of leaves, when the first heart-shaped leaf fluttered to the sidewalk before my feet, and my mind and heart went spinning back to the wonderful time when Widy graced my life. You see, Widy sends heart-shaped leaves into my path every once in a while, to draw me back to those grace filled days when his story was woven into mine. Those wonderful Widy days that filled my life with blessings, only understood over the passage of time, that were forever etched upon my heart. I would like to share with you Widy's story and how this beautiful and unique boy, bright as the sun, came into my life like a breezy kiss from God.

I think we are all inextricably linked from all eternity to all eternity. Our lives are joined in one exquisitely beautiful story of God's love. We are each beautifully, wonderfully made and we are all essential in the one beautiful proclamation of God's glory. As I have pondered the miracle of Widy, I can now see God's creative intricacies in the way He prepared the way for Widy to bless my life. Let me begin with a brief trip into my own faith journey.

"Before I formed you in the womb, I knew you, before you were born I dedicated you." Jeremiah 1:5

My life began long ago in a little town in New York State. When God created me, in my mother's womb, I was the third child of a simple, faith filled, prayerful couple. My Mom and Dad didn't understand deep theological thoughts or facts, but they deeply believed in a caring, compassionate God who calls us to be caring and compassionate to His people—all His people. God endowed me with the grace to love His created life especially in infants and children. This manifested itself in my childhood. I was the baby of the family with no little brothers or sisters to love. As a little girl I loved my baby dolls. I took them for walks in their doll carriage and rocked them in a cradle by my bedside. My vivid imagination would take them to my pretend church to show them off all dressed up. Later, my dolls were put away, but my love for children stayed within my heart, preparing me to love some special children of my own. I babysat a lot during high school and college, and cared for the children as if they were mine.

The eternal Author was at work.

I grew into adulthood developing an interior prayer life and growing in my love for serving others. I decided to pursue a career in teaching children with special needs. In college I continued to grow in faith and in my love for children, especially God's special children. Bob came into my life my junior year, and we certainly would not have been a match on eHarmony.com! But I listened to my heart and God filled us with a deep love for each other and for God. We had three children in the first four years of our marriage and I was in Heaven. I took them for walks in their carriage, rocked them in their cradle, and took them to church all dressed up.

God continued to guide us. When the Holy Spirit prompted, we moved from the little town in upstate New York where I had grown up, and settled in St. Louis, Missouri in 1970 and sank our roots into Midwest living. I began teaching elementary grades at our parish school, Saint Matthias. Bob and I participated in a Marriage Encounter weekend and grew even stronger in our marriage and in our faith. We became part of a team, sharing our faith and love with other couples. After having our first three children in four years, we had decided to put ourselves in control of our life and we entered the contraceptive lifestyle. We decided for ourselves that we did not have the time or the resources for any more children. But God never gives up on His children and He kept working within our brokenness. He picked up the fragments of our disconnectedness and infused the realization that we were not trusting fully in Him. Our story had drifted into dullness when we thought we knew better than God what was best for us. We prayed and struggled for a while and finally surrendered to God's plan for our marriage.

Eric (10-years-old), Sue (9-years-old), and Rob (8-years-old) welcomed a baby sister, Mary, in 1975. It's a good thing that God planted within my heart a deep love for children! Mary was treated like a princess by her big brothers and especially by her big sister. I took her for walks in her carriage, rocked her in her cradle, and took her to church to show her off all dressed up.

When I became pregnant for the fifth time, I began to pray that God would send us twins. The reasons are silly, but I'll try to explain. My father died when our Mary was only 9 months old. I missed my Dad and thought of him often. His name was Joseph and he always wanted a son named Joseph, but God graced him with three daughters. Now expecting again, I wanted to name the baby, if it was a boy, Joseph. But since our last baby was named Mary, it seemed somehow overly religious to name a new baby Joseph. So I prayed for twins, so it wouldn't seem so strange to name one of them Joseph. Our daughter suggested the name Jason Michael, and we agreed that would indeed be a fine name for a boy.

This was 1976, and there were no ultrasounds. But in faith, I prayed and thanked God each day for our twins. And God in His awesomeness answered my prayers. We did indeed have twins— two boys! We named Joseph Anthony after my father. Jason Michael is his twin. I should mention that there are no other twins in our family.

The twins were born premature and spent several weeks in the NICU (neonatal intensive care unit). That experience was a roller coaster ride of good days, bad days, ups and downs. As I visited them and held them and prayed for them, I watched the nurses who worked there. I noticed how loving and dedicated they were in caring for these precious, fragile, tiny babies. I tucked these memories into my heart. This was also a time for us to grow in our faith. Joseph became very sick and the doctors were not sure he would make it. I spent much time in the chapel at Cardinal Glennon Children's Hospital praying for my babies. They have a wonderful mosaic in that chapel. It shows children playing in a field and river and Jesus delighting in them. I found much comfort in that mosaic and unbeknownst to me, it would come back later into my life.

The twins finally came home and once again I took them for walks in their carriage, rocked them in their cradle, and took them to church all dressed up.

I went back to my teaching job when the twins were a year old, but in my mind I kept picturing those caring, compassionate, dedicated nurses at Cardinal Glennon Children's Hospital and those precious, fragile babies.

When my kids were all in school, I left teaching, went to nursing school, and became a registered nurse. I eventually ended up in the Special Care Nursery department of the NICU – the very same NICU our twins were in.

God continued to write our story with words of providence.

Ron and Marie Peters, friends of ours, had been foster parents for years and we had always enjoyed playing with their foster children whenever we got together. One weekend, they asked if we could babysit one of their foster babies. We babysat. Our own children became very involved in the baby's care. They really enjoyed having a baby in the house and I think the poor thing probably spent very little time in his crib. Our son, Rob, then sixteen, asked why we wouldn't consider taking care of foster children. My love of children blossomed again and we became the proud foster parents of over forty infants over the next five years. I took them for walks in their carriage, rocked them in their cradle, and took them to church to show them off all dressed up.

Working the night shift began to take a toll on my family and I began hearing the whisper of the Spirit to move on to a different job. I can now see how He was gently leading me to Widy. I took a job in pediatric home health for a local hospital and took my love of children to a new level by caring for sick children and their families in their homes where children heal best. Since my job was during the day, we could no longer take foster children and that era of our life was over. I thoroughly enjoyed my job as a pediatric nurse for six or seven years and life was good.

God began nudging my heart again, this time planting the idea to leave my dream job and start a daycare in my home. I guess He had babies out there with whom He wanted to touch my life. I began caring for infants and toddlers whose mothers had to work. Parents were comfortable with my resume as an elementary teacher and a pediatric nurse. I spent my days playing with children, rocking them, reading to them and loving them. Life was good.

One Sunday at Mass, while praying after receiving Communion, I heard the whisper of the Holy Spirit and deep within my heart and soul I envisioned Bob and me in church with a child in a wheelchair. I had no idea what this meant but it remained with me and stirred up something profound that prodded me to act upon it. I couldn't tell you whether the child was a boy or a girl, nor did it matter. I kept this whisper tucked within my heart.

Was God telling me that we should go back to taking foster children again? I was at home days now and it seemed logical that we could be foster parents again—perhaps to disabled children. I went so far as to call the Division of Family Services to find out what had to be done to get our license activated. I talked to a foster parent about the whole process. Bob and I prayed about it but for some reason it just didn't seem to be the way that God wanted us to go. It just didn't feel right in my heart.

Make known to me Your ways, Lord; teach me Your paths.
Psalm 25:4

One day while browsing in the craft department of our local Walmart store, I was approached by Linda, a member of our parish. She said she had seen us in church with our foster children. She said that she had a friend in New Jersey who knew of a little boy in Peoria, Illinois who needed a home. She said that the boy was "mentally retarded" and in a wheelchair. The hairs on the back of my neck stood up and I felt goose bumps as I remembered my heart vision. Could this be the child in my vision? Could this be the answer to my pondering and praying?

Deep in my spirit I heard a heart whisper, "This is it. This is your answer." I wrote down Linda's phone number and scurried off to find Bob in the electronics department. When I told him of the encounter, he said, "That's our answer! That must be what God wants us to do. That's Jesus—we will give him a home."

We went home and prayed. We told God that if this was indeed His will, we would call the people in Peoria and trust that things would work out. We called, things worked out, and our "Widy days" began.

> *Whoever receives one such child in my name receives me;*
> *and whoever receives me, receives not me but Him who*
> *sent me. Mark 9:37*

Anne, in Peoria, had been praying for a warm, loving home for Widy and we had been praying for an answer to our vision. Our lives were being woven together. Anne was reluctantly ready to relinquish the care of this precious child to someone who had the time and resources to obtain help for him and we were seeking the child God had for us. We tried to prepare ourselves, our family, and our home for Widy. We talked it over with our grown children, and they were very supportive and loving.

As for our house, it was not really "handicapped accessible," and we had no idea what equipment Widy would come with or need to acquire, but we said many prayers that God would provide. Anne had said that Widy could still sleep in a crib (though he was four-years-old), and she would bring one along with him. He had a wheelchair also. It was kind of like being pregnant (although without morning sickness!), planning and getting ready for our new child.

> *"Do not be afraid, for I am with you." Acts 18:9, 10*

As we were waiting and preparing, my head and heart were spinning with questions and concerns. What had I gotten myself and my family into? Could I really take care of this special child? Would I really be able to do this? Would I be able to provide the care and resources this child needs? Even though I was a pediatric nurse and had made many home visits to house-holds with handicapped children, could I do what I had admired so much in those mothers, those families? Was I capable of spending my life for this child? What if I messed up? What if I couldn't get him to eat? What if I didn't give him enough love and affection? What if I messed up his medicines? I fretted and fumed and prayed the first of many prayers to God that He help me give Widy the care he needed and the love he deserved. As I prayed I became increasingly calm and then excited about enter-ing this phase of my life.

"I wonder where we're going. Mama Anne put lots of stuff in the car and we've been riding for a long time, longer than going to the store or the doctor, I hope it's somewhere fun! Now we're stopping in front of someone's house. Someone is coming out to meet us. A lady picks me up and carries me into the house. She talks to me and seems to like me. Mama Anne is bringing my stuff into the house. Mama Anne and the new lady are talking about me. I think I'm going to stay here for a while. Please love me, new lady."

Love, Widy

I will never forget the first time I saw Widy. It was a warm spring day. I took the daycare kids outside to play before lunch and tried to keep my excitement contained. I then fed the kids lunch and put them down for a nap and waited for what seemed an eternity. Bob had stayed home from work that day for our special delivery and we waited all morning and part of the afternoon for him to arrive. It was an extremely abbreviated and much less painful labor and delivery—awaiting the arrival of this very special child.

A van drove slowly down the street and stopped in front of our house. Mama Anne had traveled from Peoria with this precious cargo and we eagerly went out to greet our new son.

I couldn't help but gasp at my first sight of Widy. His head was very big. Widy had a condition called hydrocephalus, which is translated, "water brain or head." It's a collection of fluid in the ventricles of the brain, that if left uncorrected causes the head to grow larger and larger. Oh, I had expected a big head, knowing that he had hydrocephalus, but his head was even bigger than I had imagined. But, do you know what? He was smiling! In fact, he was smiling the most beautiful smile I had ever seen.

We carried him into the house and put him on the floor with some toys. Widy could not stand or sit unsupported because of the size and weight of his head. His playground was the floor. He would roll from place to place to play with various colorful toys. Mama Anne brought in his "stuff" and we began to become acquainted with the intricacies of caring for Widy. Anne explained his medications, his health history, his food likes and dislikes and his story. With the surprising serendipity God alone can execute, He allowed our family to become forever linked to Mama Anne's family and hers to ours.

In Widy's native country of Haiti, medical care is difficult if not impossible to obtain. Widy's birth mother was very poor, but she loved her child very much. She carried him around through the streets of Haiti with a towel over his head to shield him both from the heat and the looks of horror from others. Anne was a nurse working with a wonderful group of medical personnel from Peoria, Illinois who went to Haiti periodically to serve the medical needs of the poor. Widy's mother, Emilienne, brought her precious son to these people to ask for help. The medical team determined that if they brought Widy back to the United States they would find help for him. Widy's mother agreed to the plan and voluntarily surrendered her parental rights to allow her child to be brought to the U.S. so he could have a better life than she could provide. Talk about true "mother's love!" Widy was brought to Peoria to begin his new life when he was one-year-old.

In Peoria, they obtained medical care for him. They attempted to drain the fluid from Widy's brain. It worked for a very short time before collecting again in the ventricles. They knew a shunt (the usual way to correct this condition) wouldn't work for Widy. His head had grown so big that they were afraid that a shunt would drain too much fluid and his brain would tear and bleed and he could die. They medicated him for the seizures he frequently had—caused by pressure within his brain – and took care of all his medical needs.

Mama Anne took care of Widy for four years, but with the pressures of her own life, she needed someone else to have the privilege and blessings of having Widy in their lives. He had touched Anne and her family and now it was time to share those blessings with others.

It was our turn to be blessed by this special child. Anne determined it was time to say goodbye to Widy and begin her lonely drive back home. She went over to Widy, knelt beside him (he was playing on the floor) and told him she loved him but it was time for her to leave. She kissed him and said goodbye. Widy looked up at her, looked into her eyes and said, "Thank you!" Everyone in the room had tears at that heartfelt comment from a little boy who had very little brain tissue.

We began the beautiful task of getting to know this precious child and the ins and outs of caring for him. Widy could feed himself finger foods and we soon discovered he did not like sweets. He also was not terribly fond of vegetables! Pizza turned out to be his all-time favorite.

I quickly discovered that Widy greatly disliked taking his phenobarbitol, which was in liquid form. He would spit and sputter and end up with about half his dose on him, me and on anyone or anything around him. I thought, "That's an issue that needs to be addressed."

Another issue was to find a pediatrician to treat Widy. He would need a refill on his medication soon and we hadn't had a need for a pediatrician for years. Since Widy had no insurance, and could not be covered by ours, we didn't know where to turn. Then I remembered my work in home health, and a Haitian pediatrician whose patients I had cared for. She seemed very caring and I figured that being from Haiti herself, she would consider caring for Widy for a reduced rate and help in filling his medication prescriptions until we could get him covered by Bob's insurance.

When I called and told her about Widy, she became angry when I mentioned the possibility of "free care" and she hung up on me. I was dumbfounded. I guess I thought everyone would just want to help this precious child. That was by far the biggest rejection I had ever faced, and I could hardly keep from crying!

But God works in such marvelous ways! I had hardly recovered from that conversation when my phone rang. It was my daughter saying she had received a call from someone who knew a pediatrician, Dr. Bowan, from our parish. When we called her, she said she would be more than happy to treat Widy for no payment. This was the beginning of the era of seeing God's *angels* all around us!

There have been so many *angels* in Widy's life, but I will get to them as we continue our journey through our "Widy days."

The evening Mama Anne left, Widy met the rest of his family. First to meet him was Rob, our son who was living with us at the time, working out his life after a divorce. The fact that he was staying with us would prove to be extremely helpful—another of God's providences. God continues to weave—weaving bright threads into the dark colors of life.

When Rob came home from work, he greeted Widy warmly, after getting over the shock of Widy's large head. Widy was thrilled with the attention from Rob and they immediately be-

Rob with Widy

came brothers. Rob was Widy's big brother, picking him up and carrying him for me, talking to him and "playing" with him. Later, it was Rob who carved the Halloween pumpkin with Widy, and wheeled him around the neighborhood trick or treating.

Joe was the next brother to meet Widy, and then Jay. Joe and Jay, our twin sons, quickly became brothers to Widy — helping him eat, getting him in and out of his wheelchair, and "playing" with him. Widy's favorite pastime was eating pizza while watching hockey games with his brothers. My three grown "boys" who were living with us proved to be extremely helpful *angels*.

Joe and Widy "swimming"   Jay and his wife, Jessica, with Widy

Another example of how exquisitely God weaves this beautiful tapestry we call life.

Next, Widy met our daughter, Mary, her husband Jeff, and their three children. Mary greeted him warmly and quickly became his big sister. Alex and Spencer, their sons, were more hesitant, perhaps a bit confused by his appearance and actions. But they quickly warmed up to him and eventually they all became great buddies. Their daughter, Anna, was just a little too young to warm up quickly, but eventually she became another of Widy's collection of great friends. We soon realized how very much Widy enjoyed being around other children.

Mary, Jeff, Alex and Spencer with Widy

Our older daughter Sue and her family arrived next to meet their new brother, brother-in-law, and nephew. While the oldest son, Brian, was afraid to come into the living room at first, the two other children, Brandon and Alyssa, were cautious but friendly. These three eventually became Widy's admirers and best of friends. Sue later related that Brian had a nightmare about Widy, that first night. I recently asked Brian about this, and he does not recall the nightmare nor being afraid of Widy.

Eric and his wife, Eun, were the last of our children to meet Widy. They immediately befriended him and he was then officially and lovingly welcomed into the Hauf family, a family deeply steeped in love and caring for one another. The foundation was made stronger each day by the presence of this precious child called Widy.

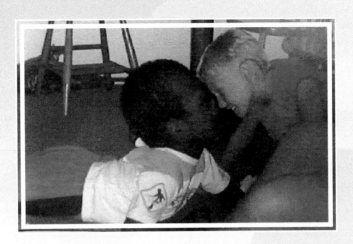

Widy and Brian. Best friends.

"I have met lots of new people today—mostly kids. I sure hope they like me. Some of them are kind of scared of me, I think. Please like me, kids."

Love, Widy

Our seven children

Lessons

I can't begin to thank God enough for the lessons He taught our children and grandchildren through Widy. He taught all of us so very many lessons. He taught them to our children and grandchildren and through them our great grandchildren, and great, great grandchildren and so on and so on and so on.

He taught all the daycare kids he interacted with all these lessons as well. He taught many people I've forgotten to mention, or perhaps don't even know about, valuable lessons about life, love, and primarily, God's love for us and His plan for each of us despite our inabilities or handicaps. Every life is valuable. Every life has a purpose in God's great tapestry of life. He taught us lessons that one could never learn from books or lectures, or homilies. Lessons that no one can "teach" us except for living the truth of God's love for us.

Specifically, he taught our kids and grandkids and the daycare kids that a child in a wheelchair is a child, just like them, even if he looks and acts very differently. They learned that he is a beloved child of God, who has feelings and needs just like any child. They learned invaluable lessons about the value of every human life. They learned that people are people, loved and embraced by God, no matter the color of their skin. They learned that each person is beloved by God no matter how different he looks or acts. They learned that every person has needs and desires and likes and dislikes and, most of all, deserves to be treated with the dignity due a child of God. They learned that no life is useless. You see, Widy with all his "disabilities" would be considered useless, a burden, and a drain on society in the world's eyes. Yet he showed everyone he met, and some he never met face to face, that God has a plan for everyone. And no one is useless. They also became aware of the many *angels* of God who travel this world with us; lessons no one can ever take away from them.

Angels all around

Widy had so many *angels* in his life, and each and every one showed God's love in a very special way.

The first *angel* in Widy's life was his Haiti Mama, Emilienne. She so lovingly cared for him, and even more lovingly gave him from her arms to those who could offer him a better life. What an expression of mother's love! Truly an *angel*!

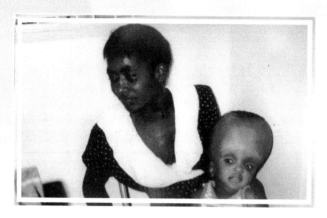

Widy with his mother

"Dear God,

Thank you for the people You put in my life.
Why did You make me this way?
Who will ever love me –the way I look?

Thank You, Mama Anne and Dr. Carroll for taking such good care for me. Thank you for comforting me on the plane ride when the pressure in my head made me crabby and irritable. Thank you for not throwing me out the window!

Mama Anne, how can I begin to thank you for all you have done for me? You love me even though I look so different and act so different. You show me how God loves—without regard to how we look or act. I am so blessed to have you in my life—to love me and care for me."

Love, Widy

Dr. Carroll and Mama Anne brought Widy to America for medical help and a better life. They cared for him on the plane ride—a ride that was uncomfortable for Widy—I bet he did have a giant headache! And Mama Anne's family helped her take good care of him and showed him lots of love and fun times. Truly they were *angels* in his life. I also understand that Dr. Carroll came to Widy's rescue many times during medical crises in Peoria. I'm sure there were many more *angels* in Peoria who are also woven into the tapestry of Widy's life.

Dr. Carroll, Mama Anne and Widy on the plane

Mama Anne and Widy

"Then, one day I remember meeting my new family and then I met new angels.

The first one I remember then was Dr. Bowan. My Mama Jody took me to see her. And do you know what? She treated me with love and caring and she didn't even charge to treat me. She knew that Mama Jody and Daddy didn't have insurance for me and they didn't have a lot of money. She talked to me and tested me, and the greatest thing she did for me was to give me my medicine in pill form that Mama could crush and give to me without my spitting it out all over the place. She also referred me to a wonderful neurosurgeon—more about him later. Thank you for Dr. Bowan."

Love, Widy

Widy had many medical concerns that needed to be addressed, and Dr. Bowan was surely an *angel* on that front. I remember distinctly the first time I took Widy to see her. It was very shortly after he first came to us. She examined him, talked to him and, I think, fell in love with him. He smiled at her, showed off his vocabulary, and responded to many of her requests.

Peoria family with Widy

Dr. Bowan said that she had patients who had tried liquid phe-nobarbitol and that it tasted worse than bad. She prescribed it in a pill form that I could crush and mix with food. Widy had suffered so many seizures in Peoria due to the fact that he spit out so much of his phenobarb, that I told Dr. Bowan that she saved Widy's life because he had so few seizures after we started giving him his medicine in pill form. She also recommended a wonderful neuro-surgeon for us to see once we obtained insurance.

> *"Thank you for sending Fred Vilbig into my life to help my Mom and Dad get custody of me."*
>
> *Love, Widy*

Widy also needed therapies and equipment. We knew that we would have to get legal custody of Widy in order to get him covered by Bob's insurance. Of course, we had no idea how to go about this. But God sent another *angel* into Widy's life. He was Fred Vilbig, a lawyer from our parish. We met with him and gave him all of the papers we had of Widy's. He did the legal work for us and contacted us when a court date had been arranged. He went to court with us, supported us, rejoiced with us—all with no financial compensation. He and his wife even sent us a cookie bouquet to congratulate us when the judgment was final and we had custody papers in hand! Isn't God awesome?

> *"There is a very special lady who was truly an angel. Bet-ty made my life so much better and even kept helping after I died. Thank You, Betty."*
>
> *Love, Widy*

When Widy entered our life, we were not equipped for getting his wheelchair around or, for that matter, for getting him around in the car. We did manage to get a booster seat that served him well and kept him safe. His wheelchair was another story. We had two cars—both sedans. Widy's wheelchair did not fold, but I did manage to find the strength to maneuver it enough to get it into the car so that I could take Widy out into the world—to the store, to the mall, to church. For the first two weeks that we had Widy, my arms were covered with bruises from trying to wrestle the wheelchair into and out of the car.

After we obtained insurance coverage, we ordered a new wheelchair. Great! It fit Widy better—in fact, it fit Widy perfectly. But It did not fold either. It was still a great hassle to get him anywhere. In order to fit the new wheelchair in the trunk of our car, we had to practically dismantle the whole thing. We had to take the wheels off, the footrest and headrest off, then fit it carefully into the trunk. Needless to say, we thought carefully before we went places with Widy.

One day, we took Widy over to our daughter Sue's house. Sue's then mother-in-law, Betty, was there visiting. Betty was touched by Widy in a very special way. She saw in him the love God has for each of us and that no matter how broken we are, we are precious in God's eyes. She saw us struggle with Widy's wheelchair and asked us if there wasn't an easier way. We said that we knew of no easier way except to get a portable wheelchair. They made stroller-like wheelchairs with the head support that Widy needed, but they were expensive and we couldn't afford to buy one. She thought for a minute, then asked, "Would you be kind enough to let me buy him one?"

It's hard to let people help you. At least it is for me. I love to help others, but it's very difficult to allow others to help me. She looked so eager to help and I knew that she would be greatly blessed in helping, so I swallowed my pride and told her that would be great if she would do that. She told me to go ahead and order one that would be appropriate for him. We did that and soon we were taking Widy so many places in his brand new blue folding wheelchair! Betty enjoyed watching Widy play with the other kids and sing with them. She was so

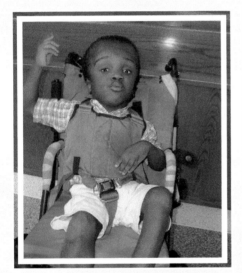 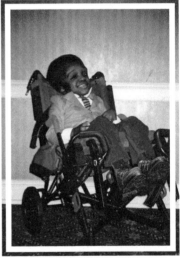

Widy in his blue stroller chair that Betty bought for him

Widy's headstone bought by Betty

happy and proud when Widy learned to say "Betty." I think Widy taught Betty a lot about God, too.

When Widy died, Betty was with us in Branson and she again asked if she could do something. She asked if she could buy his headstone for his grave. She had only one request – that it have an *angel* on it. She saw Widy as one of God's messengers, and she was the one that was an *angel* to Widy.

"I remember Chad and Heather at Bandana's Restaurant and how special they made me feel. Thank You, Chad and Heather."

Love, Widy

One of the places that Widy loved to go was Bandana's BBQ Restaurant. Our whole family would gather there every Sunday after church, and when Widy joined our family we of course took him with us. Widy loved Bandana's and not only for the great food, it was especially for the awesome people who worked there. There was a waitress named Heather. Heather was so good to Widy. She talked to him and took special care of him. Widy would break into a huge smile when he spotted her and he loved her. Heather was an *angel* in Widy's life.

Soon Heather had to share Widy. Chad, another waiter, grew to love Widy, too, and played a very important role in Widy's life.

When Heather left to go to nursing school, Chad took over completely. He always had Widy's green beans waiting when we arrived. Surprisingly, Widy liked Bandana's green beans –the only times I could get him to eat a vegetable! I really think it was because they were supplied by Chad! He would squat down to be face-to-face and talk to Widy and treated him with such dignity and caring. Widy loved him and he made Widy very happy.

One Sunday when we were in the restaurant, Chad was being his usual self—super nice to Widy. At the table behind us were two ladies enjoying their lunch. They obviously enjoyed watching Chad with Widy, and when they left, they left Chad with a big tip because he "was so good to that little boy." Little did they know that Chad was that good to Widy every Sunday. We, in fact, celebrated family birthdays at Bandana's – complete with balloons and cake. And Widy's birthday celebrations (usually celebrated with Rob since their birthdays were pretty close together) always had to include Chad at Bandana's even if we had other celebrations at home. And Chad's participation in Widy's life did not end in Bandana's. During Widy's many stays in the hospital, inevitably Chad would show up to visit and bring him some good food.

And, even then it didn't end. When Widy died and we told Chad, he went to the owners of Bandana's and asked if they could do something for the friends and family of a very special little boy. Bandana's not only supplied a feast, wonderful, top of their menu food, for friends and family after the funeral, but

Heather waiting for Widy

Widy with Chad

35

they sent it out with someone who very carefully instructed us on how to keep and serve it. They are truly a restaurant with a heart. And Chad was truly an *angel* in Widy's life.

We still go to Bandana's today and though it's twelve years later I still miss Widy and I can still "see" Widy there! In fact, one of the managers and a waitress are still there and we often have great talks—exchanging Widy stories.

"I can't forget another very special angel—Linda Ryan. She helped me find my Mom and Dad in St. Louis. She listened to God's whisper and helped me find more angels. Thank You, Linda."

Love, Widy

The first *angel* we knew in Widy's life was Linda. Linda was a fellow parishioner at Holy Infant Catholic Church and had seen us in church with various foster children. She remembered this when a friend told her about a special little boy who needed a home. She thought at least we might help her find someone. She had no idea of my whisper from God about a child in our life. As a matter of fact, she had no intention of going to Walmart that day, but as she was driving by, the thought (God's whisper) entered her mind to look there for a fabric she wanted. When she saw me (who "just happened" to be in that department at that time), she thought of her friend and that special little boy, and you know the rest. Linda was truly an *angel*.

"I really don't like having to wear only button down shirts, when all the cool kids wear t-shirts and sweat shirts and my brothers wear their jerseys to watch hockey

and football. Thank you, Marge, for helping me to dress
like a cool kid."

Love, Widy

Widy presented a problem with clothes – especially as he grew and went to school. Button front shirts weren't always in fashion – especially when going to school and trying to be "one of the kids." I could not fit t-shirts, sweatshirts or the team jerseys Widy's big brothers bought for him over his head. The openings just weren't big enough. What to do? God had the answer, of course. Enter another of Widy's *Angels*. Our son's friend, Karen, (who is now his wife) was aware of the predicament and conferred with her mother — an accomplished seamstress. Marge, Karen's mother, came to the rescue. Marge was an *angel* with a sewing machine! We would buy "school" shirts and jerseys and she would skillfully cut them down the back, fold over the edges, sew on velcro and "voila!" a shirt that could open easily to accommodate Widy's large head, then discreetly close and he looked like every other "cool" kid in school.

Watching the Blues play   Widy in his Rams jersey, ready for a game.

Widy loved watching hockey on TV with his brothers and their friends. They all wore their hockey jerseys to watch the games. Marge modified a Blues jersey for him and was he ever proud, sitting there with his brothers and their friends watching the games! We also watched the St. Louis Rams games every Sunday as a family – each with our jerseys on, so of course, Marge fixed a jersey for Widy.

Marge was truly an *angel* in Widy's life—granting him the dignity of dressing like a "regular" kid.

"Other angels I remember were the teachers, therapists, social workers, secretaries, lunch workers, students, and parents at Special School District of St. Louis County. Thank you, special angels."

Love, Widy

Widy had become an integral part of our everyday life. We soon realized that he needed therapies and help. Again, parishioner *angels* came to the rescue. Sandy and Matt Grassi led us to two very important agencies that offered help with Widy's daily living. The Special School District of St. Louis County was an amazing help enabling Widy to grow and develop life skills. The Variety Club of St. Louis was an essential resource for us in giving this wondrous child every opportunity to be the messenger of God's love that he was.

One of our first priorities when Widy came to live with us was to get him into school. He had been attending school in Peoria and Mama Anne said he really enjoyed it. When he came to live with us, I called the Special School District of St. Louis County to find out what to do. We took Widy for testing and everyone there fell in love with him. They decided he would benefit best from early childhood education classes at Southview School—the Special School District school closest to us. He would be picked up each morning by a bus equipped with a lift for his wheelchair. Thus Southview School became a huge part of Widy's life, filled with many *angels*.

Each school day morning I would sit him in his wheelchair in the front doorway of our house where he could look out and see the school bus as it approached. He soon learned to recognize that bus as it rounded the bend into our court and he would laugh and kick his leg and wave his arm—a sign he was excited and happy.

He really loved his days at school and he received many therapies there. He received physical therapy, occupational therapy and speech therapy during his school day. He loved being with the other kids and especially liked it whenever there was music involved. Widy loved music and had acquired quite a collection of CDs that he enjoyed.

Everyone at Southview School grew to love Widy and he became well known—especially for his favorite saying, "Oh, Cute", or "You're cute" – a phrase everyone thought was meant for them. Actually, Mama Anne explained that he learned this phrase on shopping trips to the mall with her and her children and grandchildren. Someone would hold up an item and someone else would say, "Oh, cute." We never told anyone the origin of that phrase. We just let everyone think he was telling them they were cute!

Special School District policy dictated that each child have an individual educational plan (an IEP), and an IEP conference is to be held at least once a year—more often if necessary. I remember sitting at a long table with 10 to 12 people discussing the best way to help Widy. I looked around at the people and thought to myself, "This is a poor child from the streets of Haiti, who if he were still there would be living on the streets, if he wasn't dead, but here he is with all of these people centered on the best way to help him achieve his very best life." Our God is awesome!

One day we received a call from the school to come pick him up because his temperature was low. I explained to the nurse that his normal temperature is lower than 98 degrees and that was normal for him. But, the district policy stated that if a child had a temperature of 95 degrees or lower they were to apply oxygen and send them home. So they insisted and I went in and brought him home. That would be the beginning of a long legal battle to allow him to attend school.

We began to get more and more calls from the school to come get Widy due to his low temperature. I would bring him home, keep him home a day or two and then send him back to school. One morning after he had been home a few days, and had been seen by a doctor who found nothing amiss with him, I had him dressed and ready for school. I told him his bus would be here soon and sat him by the front door to watch for it. The phone rang and when I answered, the school nurse informed me that Widy would no longer be allowed to attend school because of his low temperature. They sent a teacher and therapists to our home to "treat" Widy.

I was frustrated—furious that these people just didn't get it. They were a Special School District. They were supposed to provide for special children. They should be used to special children and they could not understand that Widy's temperature control was disturbed due to his severe hydrocephalus! I was beside myself! I screamed into the phone that day, "You tell this child who is sitting by the door waiting for the bus to bring him to school, which is his Paradise, that he is not allowed that pleasure!"

I slammed the phone down in that poor nurse's ear and began crying—sobbing in frustration and anger. I implored God to help this precious child. Was Widy to be deprived of the very thing that made him so happy? Why, God, would You let this happen to him? I had made a promise to Widy's Haiti Mama and to God to do everything possible to make Widy's life as full as possible.

"Now what do I do?" I asked God. Suddenly, the phone rang again. No, it was not the nurse calling to say it was all a mistake and Widy could come back to school. It was an anonymous person who wanted to let me know the existence of a Children's Legal Alliance that often helps children in cases such as this. Our awesome God didn't take long to answer my prayers!

> *Be strong and of good courage; be not frightened,*
> *neither be dismayed; for the Lord your God is with*
> *you wherever you go. Joshua 1:9*

I looked up the agency's phone number, made the call and in a few days Widy and I were sitting in their office discussing legal action to get Widy back to school. More *angels* woven into our lives. Widy was assigned a lawyer who visited the school, delved through rules and regulations, arranged meetings, went with us to a special IEP, and in general fought "tooth and nail" for Widy. The school offered and sent, as I said, teachers and therapists to help Widy at home, but Widy missed school. He missed the kids, the people interacting with him, the whole atmosphere. We finally had a big meeting with the school board president, the principal of the school, teachers, therapists, school nurses, social workers, the lawyer and us. I remember sitting there looking around the room at all these "important" people and praying, "God, this is in your hands. You know what Widy needs. Please make it happen." The district gave offers of increased in-home hours of academic instruction and therapies to which we (the lawyer and Bob and I) said a resounding NO. Not good enough – he needs to be in a school environment. I remember saying in frustration, "I don't care if you teach Widy calculus at home, that's not what he needs. We don't know how long we are going to have Widy on this earth and he deserves to have the very best life has to offer. He loves being with other children—that's what he needs. He needs to be in school." After many standoffs between the Special School District and our lawyer, it was finally agreed that we would have Widy examined by a neurologist and abide by his decision as to whether Widy should be in school or not.

We made an appointment with the neurology clinic at SSM Cardinal Glennon Children's Hospital. We still had not obtained custody or insurance yet at this point. Mama Anne drove down to go with us to the neurologist and the school nurse met us there. Widy met with the doctor and charmed him of course and gave appropriate responses, showed off his vocabulary and treated him to his rendition of "Twinkle, Twinkle Little Star." He cooperated with the doctor in the tests he did. Mama Anne and I looked at each other gleefully when the neurologist said, "There is no doubt. This child should be in school." The school nurse took notes.

The following week Widy was once again waiting at the front door for the school bus to round the corner to our house to whisk him off to his favorite place.

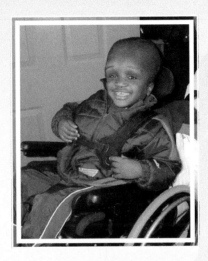

Waiting for the school bus.

School picture

Doctors, doctors, doctors

"Boy, did I give doctors a run for their money! Many had never seen anyone with a head the size of mine, or for that matter anyone with the amount of brain that I had, do things as well as I could. I really am thankful for all the wonderful doctors, nurses and therapists in my life."

Love, Widy

Dr. Bowan was the first of many medical people involved in Widy's life. You've already heard about her and the phenobarbital problem. Dr. Bowan mentioned surgery on first seeing Widy. Surgery to control his growing head. Surgery to relieve the pressure in his brain. She referred Widy to a neurosurgeon at SSM Cardinal Glennon Children's Hospital.

Once we obtained legal custody, we began the process of getting Widy covered by our health insurance. And that certainly was a process! They wanted to know why we had legal custody and what had happened to Widy's parents. They wanted death certificates for his parents. Now, remember that Widy was born in the country of Haiti. There were no birth certificates, let alone death certificates. We had in our hands the papers from Haiti that stated his mother had surrendered her parental rights to allow him to come to the United States for medical treatment for "a sick head." After many phone calls and tedious explanations, we finally convinced the insurance company to grant him dependent coverage.

We followed Dr. Bowan's advice and took him to the neurosurgeon she recommended. He was quite surprised with the size of Widy's head and even more surprised by the mental ability he had. He agreed that Widy had a life to live and he deserved to live it to the best of his ability. We gave him Widy's medical records from Peoria and asked him to help us give Widy the best chance for the fullest life he could have. After thinking about it and consulting with a plastic surgeon, he suggested surgery.

Widy had a huge fontanel, which is like a baby's soft spot. This fontanel had allowed his head to grow by two to three centimeters since he had come to live with us. His fontanel would continue to grow, as would his head, until he wouldn't be able to hold it up any more and would be confined to bed.

He scheduled a CT scan for Widy and a subsequent appointment with a plastic surgeon. Mama Anne came for that appointment, and Dr. B said that he felt surgery would be beneficial.

The plastic surgeon proposed a surgery to close Widy's huge fontanel and reconstruct his forehead to make his head smaller and to prevent further growth. Bob and I were extremely optimistic and excited about this, but Mama Anne not so, and she left troubled. She was not as optimistic as we were and neither was Dr. Carroll, the doctor who brought Widy to the U.S. from Haiti.

We received a phone call from Dr. Carroll asking us to please not have surgery, that he felt it would be too risky and would not accomplish anything significant. That threw us into turmoil. I only wanted what was best for Widy. In my prayers, I had promised Widy's Haiti Mama and Widy the best and fullest life I could provide, that I would do everything in my power to carry out God's plan for this precious child.

We talked to Dr. Bowan and she suggested we get an opinion from another surgeon. Now, if this were a fairytale, the second doctor would say that surgery was the way to go and life would be easy. But since this is real-life and not a fairytale, the second opinion was no surgery—leave things the way they are.

It was a quiet ride home as Bob and I internalized this twist and contemplated what to do next. The primary thought that I feel God placed in my mind was this – if we did nothing, Widy's head would continue to grow and grow until he could no longer hold it up. If we had the surgery, he could continue to enjoy life. But if something went wrong in surgery, he would die quickly.

I begged God for guidance and I felt in my heart that surgery was the way to go. We stormed Heaven and how I wished God would just send down a note telling us what to do. Of course, that didn't happen. So began many inner discussions about Widy, his history, his future, his life. I finally came up with these thoughts. Widy is precious. I promised him, his Haiti mama and God that I would provide the best possible life for him. With his head already having grown two centimeters since he came to us, what kind of life did I see for him? I could foresee his head growing so big that he would no longer be able to hold it up. He would be suffering from pressure in his head and even worse, he would be confined to bed and cut off from school and the social activities which he loved. He would die slowly and isolated with suffering.

If we went ahead with the surgery, he would have a chance to live the life he loved—surrounded by the people he loved and who loved him. If something did go very wrong in surgery and he died, it would be quick and without suffering. I begged God for guidance and I felt in my heart that surgery was the way to go. After all the conflict in my mind and after many prayers, I felt completely at peace with this decision.

Be strong and courageous! Do not be afraid or discouraged. For the Lord your God is with you wherever you go. Joshua 1:9

I kept a journal at this time. Here are some excerpts:

August 15
Today I called Cardinal Glennon and told them we want to go ahead with your surgery. Every time I see you with your head down or put your hand to your head and say, "ow" I feel for you. I pray each day that God will heal you and help you feel better. Do you suppose He will do that through Dr. B?

August 23
They called from Cardinal Glennon today—your surgery is scheduled for October nineteenth. I'll let Mama Anne know because she will want to be here for you, too. I'm scared, Lord. This is such a big decision. Please Lord, hold Widy in Your arms. He so precious and so loving. He speaks You to everyone.

August 29
Tonight Dr. Carroll called to beg us not to have your surgery done. He said he made a commitment to your mother to take care of you. I told him that I had also made a commitment to your mother that you would have every opportunity to have the best life possible. Dear Lord, how does one ever know which is the right path to follow? How can we know what to do? Please Lord, help us to know what to do. What path to follow. Lord, we want so very much for Widy. We want him to have every possible chance to ac-

complish his every dream. I know You have placed dreams within his heart and You will help him to realize them. Please, Lord, help us. We long to do Your will.

September 26

We saw Dr. P today for a second opinion. He said to do nothing. Don't do the surgery. Oh Lord, I am so confused! Two doctors say yes to surgery and two doctors say no. How can we know what to do? Lord, make your Will known to us. I want so much for Widy. I want him to have the surgery and feel like I've given him every chance, but if something happens to him in surgery, I'll feel like I killed him. Oh Lord, please help us!

September 27

I spoke with Dr. Bowan today. She was surprised at Dr. P's recommendation. She said she will try to talk with him and find out his reasoning and get back with us. She hopes to get the two doctors to talk and maybe through all this we can come up with a reasonable decision. Please Lord, let us do your will.

October 1

Dr. Bowan called to say that she sent an email to Dr B to discuss Widy with Dr. P to help us reach a decision. Dear Lord, will You just write us a note of what You want us to do and send it to us? We only want to do what's best for Widy.

October 4

Today Dr. B's office called to schedule your bloodwork for surgery. I told them that we are undecided about the surgery and that we needed to talk with the doctor. We just want to do the right thing for you.

October 5

Today, Dr. B called from Chicago on his way to Germany for a conference. He said that Dr. P. says no to surgery but he doesn't give any positive direction as to what to do. He suggests that we postpone the surgery for now and he and the plastic surgeon will look at your CT scan again and discuss options. He just wants so much for you. We love you so much.

October 18

Dr. B's office called – Dr. B and Dr. R (the plastic surgeon) met and discussed your case. They see surgery as a good option. They think they can help you. Please Lord, help us make the right decision, or better yet make whatever decision we make, right! Help us to do Your will.

October 23

Dr. B's office called. You have a CT scan scheduled for November 15th—-with sedation. Please Lord, protect Widy and let him be okay with the sedation. Then you have a clinic appointment with Dr. B and Dr. R. on November 16 to discuss surgery and answer questions. Your surgery is scheduled for December 14th. Lord, help us. We long to do Your will.

November 21

It's been a long time since I've written. Your teacher tells us that you are putting your head down a lot, especially in the afternoon. I wonder if your neck is getting sore or if you get tired of holding it up. You had an appointment for a CT scan last week. We got there almost late and had to wait a long time to get you in. When they found out about your previous reactions to sedation, they were really hesitant to sedate you. They wanted either an ICU doctor or an anesthesiologist there. By this time, you had been without food or drink for far too long and you were getting cold. They postponed the scan until today. Today went very smoothly and you did very well. The anesthesiologist administered your sedation and you did very well with it. We took you to Bandana's afterward and you got to see Heather and Chad. You were very happy.

And so, we have made the decision to have the surgery done. After all the conflict in my mind and after many prayers, I felt completely at peace with the decision to have surgery.

Bob's brother is a priest, an Oblate of Mary Immaculate, and his life was certainly touched by Widy as he touched Widy's life. Father Ed spends two weeks of his vacation with us every year. He has watched our children grow up and participated in their Sacraments. He has baptized most of our grandchildren. Of course, like everyone else, he became quickly charmed by Widy and cared for him deeply.

When we finally scheduled Widy's surgery, Father Ed suggested he receive Anointing of the Sick, a sacrament that imposes Jesus' healing upon the recipient. We asked Mama Anne if Widy had ever been baptized and she stated that he had. We talked with a priest about Widy receiving Communion, Jesus' Body and Blood, but he didn't feel it should be done as we couldn't tell for sure whether Widy really understood what the Eucharist was.

This was a real sorrow for me. Widy loved attending Mass with us and when we left the pew to go up to receive Jesus, he would look sad and would greet us heartily when we returned. He, of course, greeted everyone passing by in the aisle with a great big Widy smile and most people responded by patting his head or shaking his hand.

At any rate, I hurt for him because he couldn't receive Jesus to console him and strengthen him on his journey in this life. And besides, how would we know whether he understood what the Eucharist was or was not? He didn't have words to tell us.

Anointing of the sick is a sacrament that Fr. Ed felt could sustain Widy and strengthen him for his surgery and recovery. Father Ed also obtained permission to confirm him at the same time.

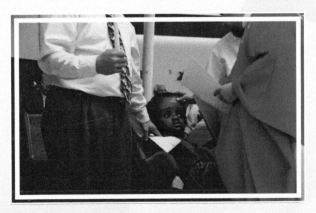

Fr. Ed anointing Widy

So, we planned a grand celebration and many friends came to celebrate this great day. We gathered in church and joyfully celebrated Widy's confirmation. Fr. Ed also administered the sacrament of Anointing of the Sick. We had an awesome party afterward, and Widy enjoyed the attention and revelry. He was shining and ready for surgery.

Before Widy's surgery, I made him a quilt. It wasn't a quilt in the traditional sense with detailed design and quilting. Instead, it was based on an idea I had read about way back when I was teaching. Back then I bought a length of white cotton cloth and divided it into squares with a pen. Each student in my class could choose six or seven squares, and with fabric markers drew a picture or pattern in each of their squares. I encouraged them to make sure their squares were in very different areas on the material. The kids eagerly embraced the project. When they had finished I placed a dress pattern on the material, cut it out and made a dress out of it. Whenever I wore it, the kids loved to look it over and point out their art work.

For Widy's quilt, I cut the white material into squares and had each person design a square. My daycare families, our kids and grandchildren, Fr. Ed, Bob and I each used our artistic talents to design our squares. Then, at Widy's confirmation celebration, I set out squares and fabric markers and invited each guest to make a square for Widy. I added a few pictures by computer-printed-transfers and then sewed all the squares together. I sewed them all together, making a sort of quilt. This way I felt like I was making a special cover for Widy. Something Widy could recognize and hang onto to give him some comfort and security when I couldn't physically be there. I wanted him to feel everyone's love.

In God I trust; I shall not fear. Psalm 56:12

The day of Widy's surgery, we got up very early to drive to SSM Cardinal Glennon Children's Hospital and Rob went with us. We checked Widy in, got him dressed in his hospital jammies, put him into bed and waited and waited. The doctors and nurses came and took his vital signs, examined him, asked a million questions, and got him ready for surgery.

Widy enjoyed all the pre-op attention and was in good spirits when they finally came in and whisked him away to the operating room. We walked with him as far as we could go, gave him lots of hugs and kisses and told him we'd see him in a little while. I don't know why, but I did not feel nervous. In fact, I felt peace.

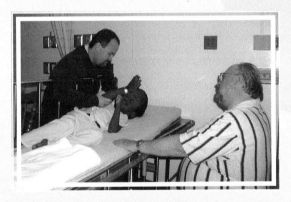

Rob and Bob with Widy waiting for surgery

That was the beginning of what seemed like the longest day I have ever had. Rob and Bob and I tried to eat something and then settled down in the waiting room for what turned out to be a very, very long wait. Mama Anne and her son arrived later in the morning and waited with us as we shared Widy stories and waited and waited and prayed and prayed. Other families were also in the waiting room and one by one they got their phone

53

call and went out to greet their children and we sat and waited and waited and prayed and prayed.

I began to fret. What had we gotten Widy into? Was this the right thing to do? Oh, please Lord, hold him in the palm of Your hand. Guide the surgeons. You are the great surgeon, the great healer. Please take care of Widy.

I couldn't help but wonder if I had wanted Widy's surgery for me or for him. I wondered if I was putting him through this ordeal because I wanted him around more for me. I love him so much! Or if it was best for Widy. I prayed that I had made the right decision and that God would continue to hold him in the palm of His hand.

Finally, we got the call that said the surgery had gone fine. Widy was doing well and it would be a couple of hours until they finished up. At last the neurosurgeon came in along with the plastic surgeon and told us that Widy had done great and was being settled in the ICU.

We immediately went down to the chapel to pray a great prayer of thanksgiving to our awesome God. It had been a very long 10 hours and we were all exhausted. Then the greatest thing of all, we were able to finally see Widy in ICU. At least they told us it was Widy.

The first glimpse was wonderful and awful all at once. It was hard to recognize him. His head was wrapped in bandages, he was on a ventilator, with a tube in his mouth, with IV lines, monitor wires, and tubes everywhere. His eyes were swollen shut and he lay very still. But he was the most beautiful sight in all the world. Mama Anne and I took turns throughout that first night sitting at his bedside, holding his hand, and talking to him.

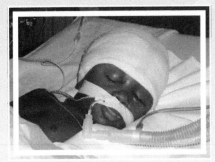
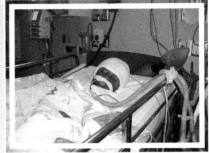

Widy, after surgery. See his quilt?

Widy's surgery was in early December and we fully expected him to come home by Christmas. He seemed to be making great progress for a while. He got the bandages off his head and I have to admit his head looked pretty funny for a while. There was swelling on one side or the other, and a big incision from ear to ear. But, there was always that Widy smile.

Widy began having trouble with the sodium balance in his body, but they finally conquered it and sent him to the regular floor. Unfortunately, he had sodium balance problems again, and ended up back in the ICU.

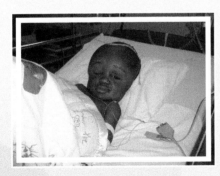
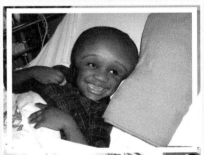

Recovering from surgery

He has his quilt.

Widy spent Christmas that year in the intensive care unit. We brought him a little Christmas tree for the table by his bed and he had his music and the videos that he loved. We took his presents to him on Christmas Eve and he had such fun with his brothers, opening them. I really think he enjoyed playing with the wrapping paper more than he enjoyed the presents!

I vividly remember Christmas Eve in the ICU. After a hilarious time of Widy opening presents and his brothers trying to convince him to play with the toys instead of the wrappings and boxes, I stubbornly insisted that I wanted to hold Widy and rock him for a while. His nurse was not overly enthused by my request as Widy was attached to IVs and monitors and a catheter, but she complied, and with the nurse's help we managed to string along all the tubes and wires that he was hooked up with and I happily and prayerfully held him for a little while and rocked him and sang to him. That was my best Christmas present—sitting in that hospital room with just the light from that little tree, rocking and singing to this precious gift from God. All I could do was thank God and sing to Widy.

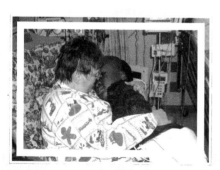

A most precious moment!

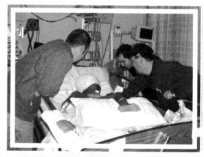

Widy and his brothers Rob, Jay and Joe celebrate Christmas

While Widy was in the hospital recovering, Heather, the waitress from Bandana's, visited him. His teachers also visited him quite often. As he got better and better and was able to begin to eat real food again, the hospital staff would put his tray by his bed and leave him to feed himself. Very often when I couldn't get in there to feed him or to help him eat, his teachers would stay and make sure he ate his dinner. Widy always brought out the best in everyone.

Widy made friends with everyone in the hospital from his doctors and nurses and residents to the families of the children he shared rooms with. In fact, they would often let Widy sit up by the nurses' station, where he would greet everyone that went by with his famous Widy smile and an occasional, "oh, cute."

Finally, the day came for Widy to come home. We packed him up, received instructions on his medicines, care and follow-up visits and wheeled him out to the car. Everyone seemed to recognize Widy and said, "Goodbye Widy, glad you are getting to go home but we'll miss you!"

Widy was known as a "frequent flyer" in SSM Cardinal Glennon's emergency room. He was sent there frequently from school due to his low body temperature and we took him there frequently for seizures, extremely low temperature, lethargy – anything that showed me something was not right with him. When Widy would get sick with a cold or any common illness, his temperature would go extremely low and he would often have seizures. I remember many nights being in the emergency room with him until the wee hours of the morning until they finally got him admitted. In time, the doctors and residents realized that Widy's temperature dropped when he was sick – it would not rise, as in most other children. Oftentimes his laboratory results were a bit abnormal, but would be fine for him. Eventually they coined the phrase, "Widy normal."

With Widy home again, life became a round of school, doctor's appointments, therapy and fun with kids in the family.

One day I received a call from Connie, Widy's teacher. She said she felt Widy was not feeling well. "Just a feeling," she said. He was just not acting like his cheerful self.

I went to pick him up from school to take him yet again to the emergency room to see what might be going on. By the time I got Widy buckled into the back seat he was crying. This was very unusual for him.

Now, let me explain to you that we had this older car that acted up a lot. It spit and sputtered and stopped. I had a cell phone but Bob didn't. I called him from home before picking Widy up at school and told him to meet me at the hospital. It was Valentine's Day, I remember. Why I remember you'll see shortly.

I strapped Widy into the car seat and started driving to the hospital. Widy's crying got louder and louder and I drove with more determination. And, of course, the car started acting up. It spit and sputtered and stalled if I stopped at a traffic light. I figured if I got on the highway and could keep going it would keep running. It started acting up on the highway so I pulled off the highway and prayed myself through traffic lights and stop signs until I finally found a good place to pull over. It was the parking lot of a very busy flower shop. That's how I remember it was Valentine's Day! By this time Widy is literally screaming in the backseat. I'm a wreck and I didn't know how to get hold of Bob. I tried calling the hospital but they were no help. I tried to limp along to the highway again, but the car just wouldn't run. Finally, parking along a side street, I called my son, Jay, with Widy screaming in the backseat and me nearly hysterical.

I was screaming in my head at God. Why would you let this happen? Why can't you let us get to the hospital and get help quickly? Please God, Widy is hurting and I'm trying to help him! Help him please!

Jay sensed he'd better respond quickly. He got into his car, drove with my directions to where we were and we put Widy in his car and took off for the hospital. In the ER, after CT scans and blood tests and medicines, the neurosurgeon pronounced him well enough to go home. Widy was quiet now – exhausted.

He seemed his old self, but a bit quieter for a few days and when I picked him up for yet another doctor's appointment, days later, his teacher again expressed concern. Widy's appointment was with an endocrinologist, Dr. V, at a different medical center. At Dr. V's office we weighed Widy – which was accomplished by weighing me first, then weighing me with Widy in my arms. We measured his height and took his vital signs. While we were waiting in the exam room, Widy began vomiting and having a seizure.

Dr. V came in and we all realized something was seriously wrong. Widy was becoming unresponsive. Dr. V quickly started an IV. We gathered our stuff and we all paraded, wheeling Widy through hospital corridors to the intensive care unit. I was praying all the way. I kept saying, God please help! What did I do to Widy by insisting on the surgery? Was that a mistake? Please, Lord, help us!

They got him settled in the ICU and sent him immediately for a CT scan. Now remember this is not SSM Cardinal Glennon where they knew Widy. They were amazed at his CT scan – remember "Widy normal" – and were figuring out what to do when they decided it best that he be transferred to Cardinal

Glennon. Cardinal Glennon sent a transport team to pick him up and they whisked him off in an ambulance, sirens blaring and lights flashing. We followed behind as best we could legally.

At Cardinal Glennon they were doing their own examination and called in a neurosurgeon STAT. I was in the trauma room with Widy when he began to have really bad seizures and spells of decreased heart rate. The neurosurgeon came in, assessed the situation and promptly declared that they had to do a ventriculostomy immediately – no time to take him to the operating room for the procedure – they would perform it in the emergency room.

The main problem was they needed to know his weight and height. But God had everything covered. No problem – I had just written down in my little book a few hours earlier his weight and height. I gave them the information and Bob and I waited in the emergency room waiting room while they put a tube into Widy's brain, into the ventricles to drain the fluid that had collected there in excess. They then left the tube in, connected to a device that measured the pressure inside his brain. They came out and told us it was done and he was resting, comfortably.

They sent him to the intensive care unit where we were able to visit him briefly. He was on a ventilator and comatose. We were devastated, yet I had a peace inside me that God was at work in all this.

Widy remained in a coma and on a ventilator the next day and when Dr. B came he gave us the "36 hour speech." That is, if Widy doesn't improve in 36 hours we will have to decide whether to pull the plug on the ventilator or not. We had called Mama Anne and she arrived that afternoon. Our kids came in and out to visit and talk to Widy. He remained nonresponsive.

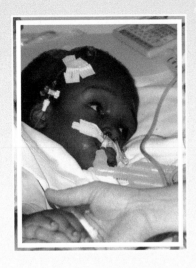

Widy with his ventriculostomy tube

Be strong, let your heart take courage, all who
hope in the Lord. Psalm 31:25

I asked God why he would lead us this far and abandon us now.
I begged him to hold Widy in his arms and kiss his poor head and
bring him back to us. A hospital chaplain came by and prayed
with us and we all told Widy to be strong, to fight, to come back
to us because we loved him so much and needed him so much.

After a few hours, as we were sitting at the side of the room
talking, we heard," Kinkel, Kinkel" (Widy's version of Twinkle,
Twinkle Little Star) from across the room. Our beloved Widy
was back! We all rushed to his bedside and greeted him. A few
hours later they discontinued the ventilator and Widy was his
cheerful self, complete with his Widy smile.

The next days were busy – normal life – me with day care,
Bob with work, and visits to Widy in the hospital. Widy was
quite a challenge to the intensive care unit staff. One time, Dr. B
came in to discover bite marks on Widy's ventriculostomy tube.

That tube goes into Widy's brain, and do you know how many germs there are in the human mouth? They had to immediately take him to the operating room to replace the ventriculostomy tube with a new one. He also was a "handy Andy" with his IV tubing and his catheter tubing, often pulling them out so that they had to be replaced.

Dr. B decided that Widy needed a shunt, but that presented a problem. Widy's ventricles were so big that if you drained all the fluid as shunts characteristically do, his brain would collapse and bleed and he would die. They searched all over the country, indeed all over the world, and found a specialized pressure-controlled shunt. When the pressure in Widy's head reached a certain point that shunt would open and remain open until the pressure reached another certain point, then it would close. Once he got that shunt in place and they were sure that it was functioning, they would send him home.

Among the visitors Widy enjoyed while he was recuperating was Chad, the waiter from Bandana's. He would bring Widy barbecue and play with him for a while. Chad said he did it because he was so fond of Widy, but I think the good-looking nurses at the hospital might have played a part! During Widy's stay we decided it best to have an endocrinologist from SSM Cardinal Glennon Children's hospital take care of Widy. Enter Dr. Dempsher.

After a few days recovering at home Widy was ready to return to school. I called the school, and arranged for the school bus to pick him up. He was ecstatic about going back to school and started laughing and kicking his leg as soon as he saw the school bus rounding the bend onto our court.

God gave us Widy, who was such a treasured gift. It was no less a gift that the toughest days with Widy were the ones through which we all grew the most. Caring for Widy was a 24-hour, 365 day a year job and here I was a 60+ year old woman who had raised six children and enjoyed her grandchildren immensely. Widy needed to be bathed, dressed, changed (as in diapers) and have medicines administered quite frequently. He also needed an advocate with school, doctors, and medical supplies. Usually I thanked God for the opportunity to perform these tasks for him. But occasionally I would begin to feel sorry for myself. I would be bathing, dressing, changing or administering and I would begin to ask God, "What am I doing here? I am an older woman who should be enjoying my golden years without these burdens and responsibilities." Then God would answer me. Widy would look straight at me and smile that wonderful Widy smile and with his limited vocabulary say, "Thank you." Thank You, God, for reminding me that fertilizer makes beautiful plants!

Being an advocate for Widy certainly wasn't easy. Getting him to school is but one example. Widy also needed advocacy in the medical field. He had really bad scoliosis due to his spine trying to support his very large and heavy head. The orthopedic doctor didn't want to do anything until Widy was older. I don't know if he didn't realize that Widy had already gone through puberty though he was only six years old. His hypothalamus and pituitary glands were compromised due to the fluid in the brain. I continued to fight for and finally won the battle to at least get a back brace for Widy. Widy of course was not so happy, but at least I felt we were doing something to stop or at least slow the curvature. On an x-ray his spine looked like an S.

Another crisis and advocacy I remember came near the end of Widy's life. Widy developed diabetes insipidus and was being treated for that. One of the things that was of extreme importance was keeping him hydrated. Getting liquids into Widy was quite a chore. Widy didn't like drinking—he disliked water, hated flavored drinks and was getting severely dehydrated. Dr. Dempsher ordered fluids, fluids, fluids. I tried to get him to drink without literally pouring it down his throat and choking him. I finally put fluids in a large syringe, stuck it into his mouth and squirted it in. He would either spit it all out all over everything or throw up, losing whatever fluids he had taken in.

I was at my wit's end one afternoon after he had spit and vomited. I implored God to help me somehow. Why God, would You bring us this far again and leave us?

Crying and pleading, I called Dr. Dempsher, begging him to help us. God planted the idea of asking for a G-tube (a tube inserted directly into the stomach through the abdominal wall) and I asked Dr. Dempsher about the possibility. He said he would call me right back. And he did—he had talked with a pediatric surgeon, and he told me to call that surgeon for an appointment.

That surgeon confirmed that a G-tube was necessary for Widy's well-being and we set a date for the surgery. The surgery went well, but a funny thing happened in the post-op area (where one recovers from surgery). The nurse came out to the waiting room and said, "I understand you have your own thermometer for Widy and you know what his normal temperature is."

Remember "Widy normal." I took my thermometer into the

post-op area and indeed Widy's temperature was normal—or at least Widy normal. Caring for Widy was not always easy but it certainly was a blessing. God really knows how to grow us in His Spirit and His love!

> *"I am the living bread that came down from heaven; whoever eats this bread will live forever." John 6:51*

Shortly after Widy came to live with us, St. Louis hosted a Eucharistic Congress. We are Roman Catholic, and in the Roman Catholic Church a Eucharistic Congress is a gathering of clergy, religious, and laity to bear witness to the real presence of Jesus in the Eucharist. Bob and I attended the event and took Widy with us.

At one of the booths we met a nun, a Daughter of St. Paul. We visited this booth with Widy because I had often taken him to their store here in St. Louis. The nun working their booth was from Boston. She fell immediately in love with Widy. She talked with him and was treated to his beautiful smile and an, "oh, cute." We told her of his upcoming surgery and our devotion to the Sacred Heart of Jesus and the fact that he always has a Sacred Heart scapular pinned to his shirt for protection—especially now with his upcoming surgery. She immediately looked in her booth and came up with a Sacred Heart of Jesus magnet and presented it to Widy. He rewarded her with a thank you smile and another "Oh, cute." Since he slept in a hospital bed which was metal, this magnet remained attached to his bed until they took his bed away after his death. Now it resides on our refrigerator.

A few weeks after the Congress was over and the nun was back in Boston, we received a letter from her. It said in part . . .

"I'm the sister who met Widy in St. Louis. I've been thinking about him often and praying for all of you. You are right in your confidence that you are living in Heaven because of Widy. He's a gift beyond words and I am so grateful to have been able to meet him and interact with him, brief as it was. There's something very deep that draws me to people with disabilities. They somehow re-veal God's face in a much more profound, pure way. They live as we are all called to live—just as being who God created them to be. And the unquestioning surrender is an example of what our own surrender to God should be. Please give Widy a hug and kiss and a blessing for me."

We met many wonderful people at the Eucharistic Congress. We met Fr. Frank Pavone of Priests for Life and Widy received a special blessing from him. Widy attended a couple of seminars with us and was very well behaved, sitting quietly, and watch-ing people. His favorite, though, was the seminar presented by Dana, a singer and staunch pro-life supporter from Ireland. We

Widy with Dana

had many of Dana's CDs at home and Widy had listened to them often, clapping and "dancing" to them. Well, when Dana started singing those familiar songs Widy really came alive, clapping and "dancing."

Dana then invited the youth present to come up on stage with her. She motioned for Widy to join them, but we couldn't get him onto the stage. We pushed him right to the edge and Dana did indeed sing to him and with him. Afterward we asked Dana if we could get a picture of her with Widy and she agreed. He of course greeted her with his marvelous Widy smile and she told him that she loved him and wished she could take him back to Ireland with her. We of course said we would never let him go.

Widy at the Eucharistic Congress

Widy was also a celebrity at the Congress. He got his picture in the weekly Catholic paper of St. Louis—The Review. It's amazing how many people reached out to Widy and we often wonder how many people were touched by Widy that day.

At the close of the Congress, we had a procession down to the Mississippi river waterfront—a Eucharistic procession, where the Blessed Sacrament is carried reverently in a monstrance (a receptacle in which the consecrated Host is held for public viewing). We joined the procession and Widy really enjoyed the singing and being with all those joyful people. We participated in Benediction—prayers said and the Blessed Sacrament revered at an altar on the riverfront. Then we all celebrated Jesus' great gift to us with an awesome fireworks display. I don't think Widy was impressed by the fireworks, but he really enjoyed being with all the people enjoying the fireworks. It was indeed a special day.

As I mentioned before, upon listening to the whisper of the Holy Spirit, I had left my perfect job as a pediatric home health nurse and started a daycare service in my home. That allowed me the opportunity to take care of Widy without worrying about getting him ready for school and home from school and being there for him when he didn't have school. I felt I had a lot to offer when I started the daycare, being a former teacher and a pediatric nurse, but little did I realize just how blessed these children would be when Widy came to live with us.

Widy just glowed with joy whenever he was around other kids. He loved to sing and "dance" with them and he was always kicking his leg with happiness when kids were around. And those kids, those daycare kids, loved Widy. They would climb on his wheelchair and sing with him. He celebrated their birthdays with them at our daycare birthday parties and loved singing Happy Birthday even though he wouldn't eat the cake!

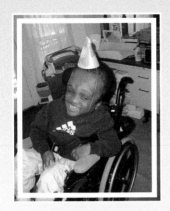

Widy helped the daycare kids celebrate their birthdays.

I once interviewed parents in regard to watching their daughter. Natalie was quite little, but gravitated towards Widy and there she was pulling herself up on Widy's wheelchair and playing with him!

The kids loved him. They saw no difference in this child who had a huge head and a different skin color, and sat in a wheelchair. They accepted him and loved him for who he was. Even though he was older in years than they were, he acted very much like them. They crawled, he rolled. They couldn't walk, neither could he. Even after they progressed beyond him in physical and intellectual development, they continued to accept him and love

An older Natalie playing with Widy   Carrie and Widy

him. He was indeed woven into the tapestry of their lives as they were woven into his.

Have I mentioned before that Widy loved music? Tunes would start and Widy would come to life. Very often when we went to our daughter Alyssa's house, her daughter would go to all her friends in the neighborhood and tell them that Widy was there. They would all come running, gather around him, some climbing up on his wheelchair, and they would enjoy a Widy songfest which always included among many songs, Widy's favorite, "Twinkle, Twinkle, Little Star." He would smile, laugh, sing and kick his leg with glee. He was in heaven.

Because of my daycare kids, I had acquired many music DVDs and CDs and Widy loved those. In particular, he loved the group called The Wiggles. The Wiggles are a group from Australia who sing, dance and in general, educationally entertain kids. Widy loved watching them, "dancing" and singing along with the videos, kicking his leg and clapping. He came to life watching them and when I heard they were coming to St. Louis, I quickly bought tickets to attend a performance. I specifically asked for handicapped seating, but when it was explained that handicapped seating was located in the balcony, I opted for regular seating close to the stage.

Our daughter, Mary, was supposed to go with us with her daughter, Anna, but at the last minute was unable to go. So, Natalie, one of my daycare kids, and her mother took their seats and met us there. The ushers put Widy's wheelchair on the side of the theater and I put Widy in the seat beside me. During the show I put Widy on my lap and we "danced" and sang throughout. He had a blast! I really enjoyed seeing this precious child just loving life! He also showed all those children around us that though he looked very different, he was just like them in loving The Wiggles. God continues to weave.

Widy loved Halloween. And not for the candy, in fact he didn't like candy and would just spit it out. On Halloween evening all the grandchildren gathered at our house for pictures, then proceeded around the neighborhood to "trick or treat." Widy loved their company and he really enjoyed himself as his big brother took him around the neighborhood.

Of course, costumes proved a bit of a problem. He went one year as a hockey goalie—with pads taped on and a stick taped to his wheelchair and the hockey jersey made to fit by Marge. Finally, another year, we found the right costume right on the department store racks. It was a piece of pizza! It would fit over his head and came complete with a "box" with an elastic strap to sit on his head. It was especially suitable since pizza was his favorite food!

Halloween with the family. Widy loved having kids around.

71

Christmas was another favorite holiday. Every Christmas Eve we went to the children's Mass. Widy loved it because everyone always made a big fuss over him. It seems that every year at least one of our grandchildren sang in the children's choir and Widy, with his love of music, enjoyed hearing them sing. After Mass everyone gathered at our house and chaos ensued. There were kids, wrapping paper, oohs and ahs, laughter and songs. Widy was in Heaven!

I struggled with what to get Widy for Christmas—from us as well as from Santa. I usually ended up with toddler toys with buttons to push—especially toys that played music. Soon however, we discovered Widy's favorite toys. One was any kind of blanket about the size of a baby receiving blanket. He would swing it by his leg and wind it around itself. He would play like that for a long while. But his most favorite toy turned out to be an empty plastic bottle—like a water bottle. He would squeeze it in his hand. He liked the crinkly noise it made and he would crinkle it in his mouth, too. Finally, he would throw it and wait for someone to pick it up and return it to him. He had all of us trained well!

Car

Getting Widy from one place to another by car was another obstacle we faced. At first he was fine in a child's car seat with a five-point harness system. But as he grew we tried booster seats with a regular seat belt, but he invariably fell over, then would be unhappy lying on the backseat unable to see out the window. We even tried a racing seat belt—a five-point harness system bolted to the car—made for bigger children. It seemed safer, but again he would fall over and be upset because he couldn't see outside.

Finally, we decided that we needed a new car. We went car shopping, and drove a sedan that Bob really liked, but realized we would have the same problem with Widy. So, we looked at minivans and Bob gave up his dream car and we bought a van. We found a company that could install lifts for wheelchairs and went out to see what was available. With a discount coupon, we got a mechanical (electrical) lift installed. We just lowered the platform, wheeled Widy onto it, then raised the platform even with the floor of the van, then pushed his wheelchair in and locked it in place behind the driver seat. Widy was harnessed into his wheelchair and with his wheelchair locked into place, we finally had a safe way to get Widy where he needed to go.

There was only one problem—if we parked in a regular handicapped spot, we didn't have enough room to lower the ramp to get Widy out or back in. And sometimes van accessible handicapped spots are hard to find, especially in places where children like to go—fast food restaurants, toy stores, parks, etc. So, I made up a magnetic sign for our side door that said, "Do not park within 10 feet of this door. Wheelchair lift in use." Not that that always worked. There were times we had to back part way out of the space, get Widy in, then proceed.

We soon discovered that one of Widy's favorite pastimes while riding in the van was to play with the top of Bob's head while he was driving.

Sundays

Our whole family met for 10:15 Mass each Sunday at Holy Infant Catholic Church. Widy loved it. Everyone greeted him and talked to him and he really enjoyed the music. He would "dance" in his wheelchair and clap if he felt like it. If it were a particularly lively song, he would really get into it and sometimes even tried to sing along. I could just imagine our loving God smiling and delighting in Widy's participation in the Mass. Widy loved the part when we greet each other in peace. He would smile and shake hands and give the occasional high five. He loved seeing people before and after Mass also.

One Sunday before Mass started, a lady came up to us and asked, "Is this, by any chance, Widy?" When we said yes, she told us she was visiting from Peoria and thought she remembered seeing him there. Well, there cannot be too many children of color in a wheelchair with a head the size of Widy's!

One Sunday, the Archbishop of St. Louis came to Holy Infant Church to celebrate Mass. We attended with Widy and sat in the front row. When Mass was over and the priests and the Archbishop prepared to process out, the Archbishop came over to Widy and gave him a special blessing. I had tears in my eyes as I once again realized just how blessed we were to have Widy in our lives.

On another Sunday, after Mass as we were leaving church, an older woman went up, right past us, stood by Widy, put her hand on his and said, "Pray for me." Then she was gone. She had realized the power and love that God has for us that Widy showed everyone every day.

Vacations

"Dear God,

Thank you for vacations. I really love it when we all get together and eat together and laugh together and most of all go for boat rides together. Thank you for the fun shows they have here in Branson. I love the music and singing and dancing."

Love, Widy

We spent our family vacations every year at a resort in Branson, Missouri. We started this tradition about eight years before Widy came to live with us. Our whole family drove down in a caravan of cars. In fact, when we first started doing this we had to communicate by walkie-talkie. Cell phones certainly made things easier!

We would check in at the resort, dock our pontoon boat, and (weather permitting) enjoy daily boat rides on Table Rock Lake. Widy was in Heaven on vacations. He loved everything about them. All the grandkids were in one place to sing with him and play with him.

Widy especially loved the boat rides. There was a path through a wooded area down a steep hill to get to our dock, so in order to get him on the boat we had to take him to a different boat dock. This dock had a ramp onto which we could wheel his wheelchair. They would bring our boat around and everyone would help Widy get onto the boat. Widy would sit by me and he loved the wind on him as we rode across the water. He loved to watch the kids tubing behind the boat, and his brothers riding their jet skis. He would laugh and kick his leg.

Widy with Fr. Ed on the boat.

On the boat.

At the resort, Widy slept in our room on the floor in a sleeping bag. We were afraid he would fall off the bed we had for him. We never knew where we would find him in the morning. He would somehow roll out of his sleeping bag and roll around the room. Sometimes we would find him halfway under our bed!

Widy in his sleeping bag.

I remember one particularly hot day on the boat. We took a long ride to enjoy a picnic in a very pretty spot on Table Rock Lake. We ate, the kids swam and took turns on the jet skis, and Widy was really enjoying himself. On the way back, the sun was especially hot. Because of his hydrocephalus, Widy's body could not control his temperature. He was getting really warm to the touch and complaining a bit—extremely unusual for him. We ended up wetting towels in the lake and draping Widy in wet towels to cool him off.

I remember one day we all went out to eat at a restaurant in Branson. There were probably twelve to fourteen of us altogether. We were seated at a long table. We placed Widy in his wheelchair at the head of the table so he could see everyone and enjoy the company. We were all enjoying our meal when BANG, we heard a thud and a collective gasp from everyone in the restaurant. We looked over at the head of the table, and all we could see were two legs and feet kicking back and forth. We rushed over and found Widy on his back with his legs and feet in the air, and he was LAUGHING. I think he thought he was on an amusement park ride, or something.

Much to the relief of everyone involved—restaurant management and employees and customers, and, of course, us—Widy was fine. His wheelchair had handles that curved out backwards like a stroller so you could push it. These handles and his padded headrest kept his head safely off the floor. He evidently had tried to push himself back from the table but his brakes held and his top-heavy head just carried him over backwards. After we picked him up and realized it was all good, we had a good laugh over those feet and legs kicking in the air. Widy really enjoyed the whole thing. But, we were very careful after that to keep a good watch whenever we put him up to the table and set his brakes!

One day I had Widy with me at the resort swimming pool. We were sitting on the ramp into the pool, in the shallow water, enjoying feeling the water and splashing. A little boy was playing nearby and I heard him say to his mother, "Look at the monster." His mother, of course, was mortified and tried to shush him. I asked her if I could talk to him and I explained that although Widy looked much different, he, in fact, was a little boy just like him. I told him that Widy liked children and enjoyed playing with and watching other children play. The little boy did warm up a bit and came closer to say "hi" to Widy and to play near him. God is so awesome in the way He instructs all of us and weaves us into His tapestry! That little boy learned a lot about

God's love and that every person is created in God's image no matter how they look.

One of Widy's favorite things in Branson were the musical theaters. We would all go to the shows and Widy would clap and "dance" through the performances. I think the family got just as much enjoyment from watching Widy as they did from the actual shows themselves.

As our vacations were "heaven" for Widy, I guess it is only fitting that Widy would go to Heaven while we were in Branson on vacation.

The beginning of the end

One of the requirements of caring for Widy was to be alert to his seizures, especially at night. His seizures were really quite mild but did involve a lot of saliva and drooling. When this happened, there was a particular danger of aspiration of the fluid into his lungs which could lead to pneumonia. Thus, Widy slept in our bedroom and I asked God to alert me in my sleep to wake up to attend to Widy.

One problem was that we had no suction equipment in the house. I raised the head of the bed hoping that would help and tried suctioning with a bulb syringe like those they send home from the hospital with a newborn. I tried the best I could, but Widy had to survive several bouts of pneumonia with antibiotics. I finally realized that we needed suction equipment at his bedside. Why I hadn't realized this earlier, I don't know. I could kick myself. We also got a heart rate monitor. That and the suction equipment really helped ease my sleep.

On Widy's last hospitalization for pneumonia (yes, even after the suction equipment), Dr. Dempsher, Widy's other doctors, nurses, and Bob and I decided that it was time for Widy to enter the "Footprints" program at SSM Cardinal Glennon Children's Hospital. That meant drawing up "do not resuscitate" orders. We agreed that if Widy were to be dying, extraordinary means should not be used.

We scheduled a conference to set up Widy in the program. Imagine sitting at a table surrounded by doctors, nurses, social workers, and chaplains discussing the death of your beloved child. Excruciating is the only word to describe it.

We all agreed that Widy should not be forced to endure the punishment of extreme resuscitation methods, nor be put on a ventilator just to keep him alive for our benefit. We stated that we wanted Widy to die at home, in familiar surroundings, with his family present, not in a sterile hospital room. We agreed on normal or ordinary means of resuscitation—CPR for a reasonable yet not extensive time, fluids and nutrition (of course), antibiotics if necessary and pain medications, and oxygen administration. We set up a time to have his "Footprints" picture taken.

A professional photographer volunteered her time to photograph Footprints kids, and she was wonderful. She concentrated on Widy's smile which, of course, was his "trademark". They also sent us home from that hospitalization with oxygen to have on hand should he need it.

An interesting aside to that hospitalization is how it happened. One day, after Widy arrived home from school, I noticed that he seemed a little "off," not quite himself. He was quiet and didn't eat well, the kind of things a mother notices when she feels her child is not doing well. I decided to take him to the emergency room to see if he had something going on. The secretaries at the desk remembered Widy ("frequent flyer," remember) but the nurses and doctors who were on duty that night were new to him. They checked him in, but decided that since he didn't have a fever he was well, and discharged him despite my objections that he was not okay. I begrudgingly took him home.

The next day, I got a call from school saying Widy was not doing well. I picked him up, took him to the ER and again they declared that he didn't have a fever (duh!) and seemed okay to them. Then Widy promptly had a seizure, complete with drooling and foaming at the mouth. (Thank You God!) They called his neurologist and endocrinologist, both of whom promptly told the ER doctors that, "This mother knows her child. If she says something is wrong, admit him immediately." I think an important lesson for residents is that every patient needs to be evaluated, not by the textbooks but by a variety of means that are individualized. For Widy, that ER visit was the beginning of the end.

In May of Widy's final days with us, our son Jay married the love of his life, Jessica. Widy, attired in a suit and tie, attended the wedding. This was not long after Widy's final hospitalization with pneumonia and he was still a bit under the weather. I was sure that at the reception Widy would come back to life and be our old Widy again. There were lots of people, lots of kids, and best of all, music and dancing. Usually when music and dancing were involved Widy would really come alive. Widy loved being on the dance floor "dancing" in his wheelchair with whomever would dance with him – usually me.

But this day, it was not to be. I took him out on the dance floor, but the sparkle was gone and as I moved him around and danced around him, he just sat there trying to smile. I was crushed and started to believe that maybe Widy was getting tired and beginning to get ready to return to his reward in Heaven. "NO," I screamed internally. "I love him too much. He still has much to teach me."

After the wedding, we realized that Widy would not be able to attend summer school. He was too sick and fragile. He spent most of his days sitting in his wheelchair, wrapped in a blanket because his temperature was lower than Widy normal. I constantly watched his heart monitor and when his heart rate went low, I would call the doctor. After a time, the doctor asked me if I remembered our Footprints contract and what we had decided about Widy's final days. Of course, I remembered, but I didn't want to give him up.

Soon after, the medical equipment company came and took back the heart monitor. I can't begin to tell you just how scared that made me. I felt completely out of control and very vulnerable. It's like I would say, "Jesus, I put Widy in Your hands." Then in the next minute I would take him back again and say, "But I can take better care of him than You can." Pretty arrogant and dumb, huh?

Widy did okay with feeding himself, but I resorted to giving him fluids by his G-tube to supplement his intake. He seemed to be getting better, so we decided to go ahead with our vacation plans to go to Branson with the whole family.

We packed Widy up for vacation, taking along a canister of oxygen as a precaution. He seemed better the morning we prepared to leave. As we departed for that last Branson vacation, we knew Widy was feeling better because he was swinging his arm and kicking his leg. Unfortunately, Bob's priest brother, Father Ed, got caught in mid-swing of Widy's arm. He said he saw stars!

As we caravanned from St. Louis to Branson, we stopped in the city of Rolla for lunch. I noticed that Widy was breathing hard. He didn't eat well, so I fed him by G-tube and we put oxygen on him. He rested comfortably for the rest of the trip.

We arrived in Branson and settled in. We continued our practice of taking Widy with us wherever we went—shopping, boat rides, shows, restaurants. However, he became increasingly less alert and more lethargic. His meals were all by G-tube now and after one intensely worrisome meal in a restaurant, with Widy seeming to drift in and out of consciousness, we decided no more outings for Widy.

He stayed in bed in our resort cabin listening to his music, with our kids and grandchildren and other family members and friends visiting to talk to him and sing with him. It was hard for the family members and friends to see Widy like this, so the visiting declined a bit. I spent my days sitting by his bed, playing his music, changing his position, feeding him, massaging him, talking and singing to him–in general, loving him and caring for him.

We soon realized that we had not brought enough oxygen with us. At home we had an oxygen concentrator (a machine that somehow takes room air and concentrates the oxygen to the level you set). Our son Jay and his wife had not yet left for Branson, so we called them and told them to go by our house, pick up the concentrator and tubing, and bring them down with them.

Whenever we tried to remove Widy's oxygen tubing, his breathing became labored. We frantically tried to find more canisters of oxygen. We tried the hospital in Branson but they could not help us. There were no medical supply places in Branson, but we finally located one in Springfield, about fifty miles away. I called and explained the situation and they sent someone out immediately.

When the person from the medical equipment company arrived with the canister, he took one look at Widy and asked when the concentrator would arrive. When I told him that it would be a day-and-a-half, he said that one tank would not be enough, and he brought in two more. That man was surely sent by God, another of Widy's *angels*.

Those final days in Branson were a true blessing. I sat by Widy's side by day and slept at his side by night. God gave me the chance to see how rewarding unconditional love is and I am forever grateful for that.

Bob was an *angel* during these days. He was concerned about me, worried about Widy and trying to rest and recuperate from a job that was, to say the least, extremely stressful and destructive for him. I know he needed me, too, but he readily gave up his needs so that I could give my all to Widy in his last days. I know that Bob was grieving also and quite often felt pulled in two directions. But God somehow let me know that Widy needed me and He strengthened and loved Bob so that he could be okay until my concern could turn to him.

Widy's last day

My soul is weary with sorrow; strengthen me according to your word. Psalm 119:28

I remember well the day that Widy went home to God. It started out like the other days of that unforgettable vacation. I woke up, changed and washed Widy, changed his position in the bed, and best of all, hugged and kissed him. I started his music and sang to him for a bit, then fed him through his G-tube and gave him his medicine. I then joined the others for breakfast.

I have no idea what the others did the rest of that day except for occasionally peeking in and checking to see how Widy was doing. I think most of them went swimming and may have gone out in the boat. I sat by Widy's bedside changing him, singing to him, giving him his medicine and changing his position, and reading my book about Silver Dollar City.

The day before, I had gone to Silver Dollar City with Eric and Eun. I felt anxious the whole time I was there. I was so afraid Widy would die when I wasn't by his side. But Eric and Eun had really wanted me to go with them and everyone was encouraging me to get out of that room for a while. And so I went, but my emotions were all over the place that day. There was a parade with lots of color and music and action, and I immediately thought, "Widy would love this." I could picture him clapping and laughing and kicking his leg like he does when he's happy. Then reality would slap me in the face and I would get incredibly sad and want to cry. Mostly, I wanted to cry out, "Let me out of here! Let's go home!" It seemed that we were gone for an eternity and on the ride back to the resort, I vowed I would not do that to myself again.

That's why the next evening when everyone was going out to dinner, I refused to go. I know that Bob really wanted me to go, and everyone else was encouraging me once again to "get out of the house for a while," but I stood my ground. I didn't like the way Widy was breathing and I just couldn't stand the thought of another anxiety-filled outing. I think God was whispering to my spirit to stay with Widy. So, I asked them to bring me home some dinner and off they went.

The next few hours were the most intense I can remember since our twins were in the neonatal intensive care unit. Shortly after everyone left, I changed Widy and turned him toward me in the bed and noticed his breathing was even more labored and uneven. He began to have spells of apnea — not breathing — and I could hear what we nurses often call a "death rattle." I picked up my cell phone and dialed Bob's number. It went immediately to voice mail.

"NO!" I screamed into the phone. I had to get hold of these people! Widy was dying and they would want to be here. I tried Ed's phone — again, voice mail. I threw the phone across the bed in utter frustration, unable to hold back the sobs now. I picked up the phone and dialed Bob's phone again. It went to voice mail right away. I tried Ed's phone again — voice mail!

Ed's voice mail message is long and seemed especially long that day as he explained that he couldn't take my call right then, but I could leave a message and phone number and he would return my call soon, then added, "God bless you."

I found myself yelling into the phone, "SHUT UP!" The message finally ended and I screamed, then sobbed into the phone, "Please come home right away. Widy is dying. I don't know if you'll make it home in time!"

Then I turned my attention to Widy, who was struggling to breathe. I held him, sang to him, and told him that if he was tired and wanted to go to Jesus, that's what he should do. As I sat there, holding him, his favorite music playing, I could only pray that he slip softly and gently into God's waiting arms.

Widy took his final breath and his life of struggle was over. Through my sobs of desolation all I could do was to thank our awesome God for letting me know this precious child.

There is an interesting story about Fr. Ed and Widy's last days. Father Ed went with us on our yearly family vacations to Branson and of course was with us the year that Widy went to Jesus. While on vacation in Branson, Fr. Ed would say Sunday Mass for the family in our resort cabin. That Sunday of Widy's last trip to Branson, we all knew that he was not doing well at all. I think we all felt that the end of his earthly journey was near, and Fr. Ed felt the call of the Holy Spirit to give Widy Holy Communion. Widy could no longer chew or swallow, but he had a G-tube through which he was fed. Fr. Ed administered the precious Blood of Jesus into his G-tube. The miraculous thing about all this is this: Widy had been hovering between life and death for days, we had stopped taking him out, and I had stayed near him at all times waiting for the moment of death. Well, Widy received the Precious Blood of Christ on Sunday, and he went home to Jesus on the following day, Monday, peacefully with a smile on his face. Was he just hanging on to life waiting for Jesus? I believe so.

The rest of the family finally arrived back home after listening to my frantic voice mail message, and telling the restaurant to make their orders "to go." Ed immediately grabbed his blessed oil and anointed Widy. Bob came in and we held each other and said goodbye to Widy as we cried together. Then followed each of our children and grandchildren to say goodbye to Widy. Each kissed him and told him goodbye. Each with tears and grief. All except the littlest grandchild who was barely two years old.

We all thanked God for sending Widy into our lives.

Now we were faced with what do. We were in Branson, five hours away from Widy's doctors and hospital. I called Dr. Dempsher, who was unable to direct us. The people in the office of our resort called the coroner of that county. Soon the coroner arrived, with a detective. We had Widy's "do not resuscitate" papers and end of life plan and presented them. The detective told us that he was there only because the law states that he has to investigate deaths in places other than hospitals. He said that Widy was obviously well cared for and the investigation and pictures he had to take were mere formality. The coroner and the detective were very compassionate and gentle in gathering the necessary information.

Then they said that it was time for them to take Widy. They suggested we might want to go somewhere else while they took his body out. I immediately sobbed with the thought running through my mind, "Widy will be all by himself tonight." I had been sleeping close by him these past few nights and couldn't bear the thought that he would be all alone. I tried to tell myself that Widy was definitely not alone, that he was with God and the angels and very probably with his "Haiti Mama" and not in that empty shell, but my heart was too heavy with grief to grasp that.

Bob and I went up to another cabin at the resort where other members of our family were staying, and when we got back to ours, the kids had already moved all of Widy's things into the trunk of our son's car. Our room, and our cabin, seemed so empty.

I decided I would love to go out in the boat. It was sunset and sunsets are so beautiful on the lake. I thought it fitting, as this day seemed like a sunset on a very beautiful part of my life. However, when we got in the boat, it wouldn't start, so we watched the sunset from the dock and decided to go out the next day after the boat was fixed.

The next day dawned bright and sunny. I was on the phone all morning with people in St. Louis. I called the funeral home, Widy's school, my daycare moms, Cardinal Glennon Hospital, everyone concerned with Widy. The hardest call was to "Mama Anne" to tell her that our precious child was gone. We grieved together and I promised to let her know of the funeral plans. Then our family went for a boat ride, which was bittersweet. I liked boat rides, but this one had something missing—Widy's happy eyes and bright smiles as we rode across the lake.

On the way back from the boat, as we were walking from the dock to our cabin, I was listening to our grandchildren talking and walking in front of us. It was one of those gorgeous, bright sunny days with beautiful blue skies and big puffy white clouds floating by. I heard one of the grandchildren say, "I bet Widy's up on one of those clouds dancing and singing." The others chimed in, "Yeah, you're right, and now he can really dance!"

Lessons learned from children!

When they released Widy's body from Branson and took him to the funeral home in Ballwin, we left Branson to return home. The people at Schrader Funeral Home were the most compassionate, caring people. They had a beautiful casket made for a child and we were grateful that the cost was not exorbitant, but reasonable. They understood our financial dilemma—no life insurance for Widy, medical bills, etc. and they worked very compassionately with us.

A Catholic cemetery in St. Louis provides a burial plot for a child free of charge. Resurrection Cemetery arranged for a beautiful spot on a hill right by a statue of our Blessed Mother Mary.

We scheduled Widy's viewing to be on Sunday with his funeral on Monday at Holy Infant Catholic Church. That Sunday morning, after Mass and lunch, we went to the funeral home. The family always gets private time with their beloved before the actual viewing time begins.

I remember standing outside the closed doors anticipating seeing Widy again. But when the doors opened I was unprepared for the barrage of overwhelming grief that prompted me to gasp, "My baby!" Bob held me and we walked up to the casket. My heart was breaking. After my initial shock of grief from seeing Widy after a few days, I was grateful for the dignity and compassion with which he had been, and continued to be, treated.

There he was, in his suit and tie—my precious Widy, resting quietly. The only thing missing was his Widy smile. But, I was sure God was enjoying that Widy smile now!

A lot of people came to say goodbye to Widy that day. His Peoria family came, of course, and there was much grieving and many tears on their part. Poor Mama Anne, she had to say goodbye to Widy again. She had had to say goodbye when he came to live with us, and now she had to say a final goodbye. The Peoria family brought pictures of a younger Widy for people to see.

So many people came to the visitation! Among them, our friends from church, the parish priests, Doctor Dempsher, the nurses from Cardinal Glennon, the teachers from Widy's school, parents of the children in Widy's school, and the parents of my daycare kids. They all came to see that precious child from Haiti who had taught us so much and showed us how God loves. One of my daycare children even brought a flower that she placed in his casket.

During his life, Widy found it very funny and would laugh whenever someone would drop something. When Mary's family came in for the viewing, her son, Spencer, brought along his Nintendo D.S. He dropped it right in front of where Widy was resting. We all agreed Widy was enjoying a laugh with God.

It was a very long day, but a beautiful day. We remembered the fun times, and the not-so-fun times. Through it all, we thanked God for allowing Widy in our lives.

The funeral the next day was a happy-sad affair. The Mass was beautiful and emphasized again the placing of Widy into God's loving arms in Heaven. Father Ed celebrated the Mass, of course, with the priests of Holy Infant concelebrating. In his homily, Father Ed stated how Widy showed us all how much our God loves us. He said that in Widy's mere nine years of life, he had touched more people's hearts than he had in his forty years of being a priest!

Our sons and sons-in-law were the pallbearers. I can remember saying to them as they carried Widy up that gentle hill to his final resting place, "One last time—you are carrying Widy to bed one last time." We had the ceremony and as I touched his casket, I begged God to heal the hurt in my heart.

"No tears for me
I am running and jumping
Skipping and laughing
Jesus at my side
The Blessed Mother smiling,
The Father enjoying,
The Spirit sparkling all around."

Love, Widy

Epilogue

Relieve the anguish of my heart, and set me free
from my distress. Psalm 25:17

After Widy

After Widy's death, I felt a need to forgive. To forgive Widy. And to forgive God.

I guess it was one of the stages of the grieving process. Forgive Widy for dying? Why? And how? Widy didn't choose to die, but he did and he left me wondering—how could you leave me when you were teaching me so much about life and God? Now who's going to teach me? Now who's going to show me God's love and graces in action?

And God—how could You do this to me?—to the world? To take from me the very person who shows me who You are?

Now, I knew in my head that Widy didn't choose to die, nor did God "take" Widy from me, but in times of grief and desolation, my heart saw it that way.

I came to realize that God teaches us and shows His love in many ways. One way He does this is through other people. He may teach or show through a great wave like Widy and his life, or it may come in ripples like a smile from someone when you feel really down, and in need of God's touch. Or it can come in a hug from someone—your child or a friend. Or, when your child posts on Facebook, "I only wish I could be half the person my mom is. Thank you for being my Mom."

God graces us with His love when a scripture passage touches you; or when something said in a homily speaks to you; or you see a couple married over seventy years receiving a special blessing and you want to cry with the beauty and depth of God's love for us.

I do forgive you, Widy.

I do forgive you, God.

I still do miss you, Widy. And I still love Widy.

Widy lived but a brief time, almost nine years, but he touched so many lives. Clearly, he is a golden thread woven into God's tapestry, there to brighten the tapestry, to brighten our lives with God's love and light.

When Widy died in Branson I insisted that I was not going to ride home with an empty wheelchair. We asked the owners of the resort if they knew of a charity to which we could donate the chair, as it was an expensive one, a good one. They found a charity and we left the wheelchair at the resort with the owners.

A few weeks later, we received a letter from the charity in Branson. The letter thanked us for the donation of the wheelchair, and said that because of that wheelchair, a little boy was now able to attend school. Widy's legacy lives on.

In the days following Widy's death, submerged in darkness and grief, I created a scrapbook of Widy's life and it helped me to cope. The Special School that Widy attended has a custom of planting a tree on their grounds in memory of a student who has passed away. On the day of Widy's tree planting ceremony, I brought my scrapbook and the principal, the teachers, the aides, and the secretaries looked through it and we all laughed and cried together.

Not long after the funeral, Jim and Nell from our church came over to just sit with me and let me talk about Widy and how special he was. They could relate, as they had also lost a child earlier in their lives. They knew the hurt and grief I felt and it gave me comfort to know they cared enough to reach out to me. And they could legitimately say, "I know how you feel."

They did not tell me that things would get better, that life goes on, that I have to get on with life–things I've heard from some well-meaning people. Jim and Nell just sat with me, cried with me, and let me go on and on and on about Widy.

Years later, remembering how Jim and Nell had ministered to me, and recalling vividly how Widy ministered to me with his life, I heard the Holy Spirit "whisper" to me in prayer about becoming a Stephen Minister. A Stephen Minister will just be there for another person as they struggle with a life event. They don't offer to fix anything or change anything, but they are just there to be there, to stand with the person and reflect God's love. I went through 50 hours of training and became a Stephen Minister. Just as Jim and Nell were there for me when Widy died, I have been there for others over the past four years. Through this ministry, Widy continues to touch the lives of others.

Bob and I became part of an international group called Teams of Our Lady. We meet monthly with other married couples for dinner and sharing. We share our Catholic faith as well as common concerns and joys. We support one another as we strive to live out God's plan for our marriages in today's culture. Since Bob and I have been married for 53 years, our contributions are very often, "You will live through this." Actually, we have learned much from these younger couples that has strengthened our marriage. At first, I wondered about joining this movement, but I really believe it was Widy's whisper, "You are never too old to learn more about God" that brought us into this wonderful group that teaches us about God.

Through the years I have taught various religion classes in our Parish School of Religion, and I have shown the students a video slide show of Widy's life story. Afterwards I ask them what was significant about Widy to them. They invariably say things like, "He's always smiling." "He seems so happy even though he is disabled." "He seems very happy and peaceful just to be as he is."

I sometimes wear shirts and sweatshirts with Widy's picture on them. It's great, because people ask about the story behind his picture, and I get to tell even more people about Widy. One of the shirts is particularly special. It was my Mother's Day present from him when he was in school. It features his picture, complete with his precious smile. Above the picture is printed, "My Mom is the Best!" And under the picture, it says,

"Love, Widy."

About a year after Widy's death, we went to Naples, Florida. One evening we were looking for a place to eat, and we spotted a store called, "The Lady from Haiti." We looked at each other and knew we had to go in!

The store owner was a woman who had taught in Haiti for a number of years and had adopted a little girl from there. That little girl was now a teenager and the woman's store was filled with trinkets and artwork from Haiti. We shared pictures of Widy, and even showed them to some customers who asked to see them. Widy's story was once again told and everyone marveled at his beautiful smile.

We brought home a star on which is Widy's name, written in gold, and two little *angels*, one made out of straw and the other made out of cloth – my Haiti *Angels*. They are a part of my prayer table along with a candle, a statue of Mary that we bought at the Lourdes Shrine in France, and a statue of the Infant of Prague. Not a day goes by that I don't think of our precious gift from God and how much I still miss him.

Before a recent service at our parish, I was talking to a woman I had just recently met. The subject of Widy came up because the woman, Sharon, had just returned with her daughter from a youth group mission trip to Haiti. I briefly told her about Widy and we went into the service. A few weeks later, after Sunday Mass, Sharon said she had something she would like to give me. She placed into my hands a pouch in which was a Rosary. She told me that it was made in Haiti and while she was there, she purchased some for her daughters and herself, but for some reason was impelled to buy one more. She said that when we were talked at that service and heard Widy's story, she knew internally why God had her buy one more Rosary. And she wanted me to have it. So now when I say my daily Rosary, I feel like I have Widy at my side.

A couple of years ago, our days with Widy inspired Bob and me to participate in the annual National March for Life in Washington D.C. We took the long trip on the Missouri Right to Life bus, two seventy-somethings with forty-eight other people, none of whom we knew. I wore my shirt with Widy's picture on it and, of course, people asked who he was and why I was wearing it. So, once again, Widy's story was told and retold and people were touched by the great love God has for us, as imperfect and broken as we are. And that He has a plan for each of us.

Widy made me even more pro-life than I was before he came into our lives. He has helped me see the dignity of all human life, and that God has a plan for all life from conception to natural death, even if that life has disabilities or infirmities. When we destroy life, we are destroying God's plan. Not a day goes by when I am not grateful for the beautiful life of Widy.

> *"I asked God to let you see me in your dreams so that you would know just how happy and loved I am here with Him. I hope you enjoy the dreams and feel my love and joy."*
>
> *Love, Widy*

One night, I had a wonderful dream about Widy. I was in the kitchen and he came walking out of the bedroom. He and I talked about what we would do that day and I hugged him and told him I loved him soooo much. He hugged me and told me he loved me. Then we were in the car, on the way to a doctor's appointment. It seemed we were always in the car heading to a doctor's appointment. When we arrived at the doctor's office, we signed in, they gathered Widy's huge file, and we sat in the waiting room just sitting next to each other, enjoying being together. Finally, they called us in and I told the doctor just how well Widy was doing, and noticed that he looked at me a little funny. Then he asked me to come into his office alone, without Widy.

As I sat in front of the doctor's desk, a strange feeling came over me and I realized that this was not one of Widy's doctors. It dawned on me then what was happening, and I said to the doctor, "I'm the only one who can see him, aren't I?" The doctor shook his head "Yes," then said, "But that's okay. Just enjoy being with him while you can." I woke up shortly after that, but the euphoric feeling remained with me for a long time. I really wish I could put into words the wonderful feeling of awe and wonder I experienced in that dream while I was with Widy. Truly I had a glimpse of Widy in Heaven with our God.

I hope that through this book, Widy continues to touch lives and perhaps, to enrich yours. Remember how God allows memories of Widy to bring me a smile when I see a heart shaped leaf? Maybe God will blow a heart shaped leaf your way today. He might be whispering to you too.

Our God is awesome and He writes each of our stories with special blessings, hidden graces and sparkling surprises. Might there be a *Widy* whom God wants to write into the story of your life?

Events in Widy's life

August 11, 1995	Widy born in Haiti
Sometime in 1996	Widy seen in Haiti by Dr. Carroll
	Widy's mother surrenders her parental rights
	Brought to Peoria, Illinois by Dr. Carroll and Mama Anne
September, 1996	First surgery, in Peoria—unsuccessful
1996 to May 2000	Widy lives in Peoria with Mama Anne and her family.
May 2000	Widy enters our lives
July 2000	Widy's first family vacation with us
Fall 2000	Widy starts school in St. Louis Special School District
March 26, 2001	Legal custody awarded to us
Spring 2001	Confirmation and anointing of the sick by Fr. Ed
April 2001	Widy's first Variety Club telethon
May, 2001	Family pictures taken
June 22, 2001	Widy attends the Eucharistic Congress with us
July, 2001	Family vacation in Branson
December 14, 2001	Widy's first surgery in St. Louis
Christmas, 2001	Widy still in hospital—in intensive care unit
February, 2002	Widy back to school
March 6, 2002	Widy sick at Dr. V's office, transported to hospital by ambulance

March 6, 2002	Ventriculostomy placed in emergency room
Spring, 2002	Widy at Variety Club Telethon
July 2002 and 2003	Family vacation in Branson
August 7, 2003	Seeing Wiggles at the Fox Theater
May 14, 2004	Jay and Jessica's wedding
July 2004	Final Branson vacation
July 5, 2004	Widy goes home to Jesus

Love

whispers

to you

MATER
MEDIA

The mission of Mater Media, the not-for-profit dedicated to Mary, the Mother of God, is to inspire people to love God, and to motivate them to serve Him. Through spiritually energizing events and innovative storytelling, Mater Media uses the power of parable to pierce through the cultural darkness and shine as a beacon of God's love and JOY!

matermedia.org